AZ0026

GreenTea
with GINSENG

壽 禺

D0384512

KEEPING HOUSE

KEEPING HOUSE

Hints and tips for a clean, tidy and well-organized home

Cindy Harris

RYLAND PETERS & SMALL
LONDON • NEW YORK

SENIOR DESIGNER Toni Kay
COMMISSIONING EDITOR Stephanie Milner
PRODUCTION David Hearn
ART DIRECTOR Leslie Harrington
EDITORIAL DIRECTOR Julia Charles
PUBLISHER Cindy Richards
INDEXER Vanessa Bird

This updated edition published in 2015
First published in 2004
by Ryland Peters & Small
20–21 Jockey's Fields,
London WC1R 4BW
and
341 East 116th Street
New York, NY 10029
www.rylandpeters.com

10 9 8 7 6 5 4 3 2 1

ISBN 978-1-84975-666-2

A CIP record for this book is available from
the British Library.

CIP data from the Library of Congress has
been applied for.

Printed and bound in China

Note

Every effort has been made by the author and the
publisher to ensure that the information given in this
book is complete and accurate. This book is not
intended as a substitute for the advice of a qualified
professional. Neither the author nor the publisher
shall be held responsible for any loss, injury, or
damage allegedly arising from any information
or advice in this book.

Contents

Introduction

The pace of our lives changes constantly. Fifty years ago, life unfolded into a single, straight line. If you were a man, you went into a career that was clear and well defined; you married one person and remained married, had children, and sent them to the local school. If you were a woman, you took care of the house, cooked the meals, raised the kids, and were the person responsible for the family's social life. But in our topsy-turvy world, the man is as likely to be the child-rearer and the gourmet cook, jobs change every few years and careers are defined by ever-evolving job titles such as 'digital co-pilot' and 'creative executive.' As the environment around us changes, what keeps us grounded? The answer is our home. Not our house – that's nothing more than rooms with furniture scattered around. Our home.

Our home is the place that most clearly reflects who we are. If you live alone, it's where you feel comforted by its very walls. Every home I've ever lived in was my haven, my special place. I've put my own distinct accessories in the bathroom to give it personality, nurtured flowers on windowsills, and cleaned taps/faucets to make them shine and make me feel good when I entered the kitchen. These are the unique touches that we put into a home.

Today, who has time to worry about how to clean silver, or where to find that unique brand of stain remover? Most of us don't know the intricate ways to maintain our home in tiptop shape. My mother, who came from a rural community, knew a hundred methods for the upkeep of fine wood; she knew about the shelf life of food, had her poultices to remove stains and easy ways to fold sheets and make the bed. She taught me how to keep a family together through careful planning and artful household 'tricks.' She always had a quick method for disposing of chores so that we could all sit around the table and tell stories.

Later, as the divorced mother of two young boys, pursuing an advanced degree and holding down a day job, I had about as little free time for housekeeping as I did for embroidery or pottery glazing. Yet your home is your temple. It is your retreat, the 'you' you present to the world. Keeping it clean, well organized and always welcoming to your family, your friends and to yourself after a hard day, is essential to a well-lived life. My mother's lessons came in handy, not just for me, but for my friends who asked for advice.

When I married a business entrepreneur who entertained on a regular basis, I had to develop a whole new set of skills. That's when I realized that the English language possesses a thesaurus for looking up words, but there is nothing like it for the homemaker – no simple guide to show us, in quick, easy-to-read bullet points, how to keep our home gleaming in the minimum amount of time, so we can still sit back and enjoy the results.

The key is being organized, and making it simple. Whether your home is a vast estate, an old family home, a small apartment, a first home or a tiny cottage somewhere in the countryside – it's your very own space to care for, no matter how large or small. Making it easy to keep clean, and take care of, can be a joy. It's one of the pleasures in life.

CLEAN HOUSE BASICS

Your home should be a place in which you can relax, feel comfortable and restore yourself from the stresses and strains of the day. Only by keeping your home in tiptop condition can it become a refuge for you and your family. A neglected home becomes a chaotic and unhappy place. A well-kept home will improve your mental well-being — if your home is in order, the rest of your life will feel manageable.

Simple home management

Your home is your castle and you are the master of this domain. This thought may be overwhelming, but it needn't be. Just follow a few simple rules for establishing an orderly routine that will turn housekeeping into an art form. Establishing priorities and setting realistic goals in your daily schedule is essential. Clean the rooms in which you spend the most time and those where cleanliness is a priority. You can let everything else go, at least for a while. Write down what needs to be done that day, do it, then check it off on your list.

HOUSEKEEPING: A STATE OF MIND

If you can change the way you think around the home, you will save yourself a lot of time and effort keeping house. Adopt these key attitudes and you and your home will instantly benefit.

Live tidy

Make this your new mantra, a state of mind to become a lifestyle! Do not let things accumulate on countertops, tables or in the sink, but put everything in its place as you go along. Put soiled clothes in the hamper and hang up all clothes as soon as you've taken them off (if they are still clean). Avoid the urge to drop or put things down where they don't belong, and don't let your family do it either. By leaving them, you create a mountain of work for yourself.

Do it now, not later

Put away newspapers, magazines and similar items as you go along. Don't leave it for later in the day. It will always look worse then. Later can easily become tomorrow, or the next day and then next week – resulting in a pile of mess and chaos.

Think ahead

An essential rule is to keep a list of supplies that you need to buy, which can be added to when you see that you've run out of something – or ideally, before you run out. There's nothing worse than realizing you don't have essential supplies at 10 o'clock at night!

Declutter your space

Before you even begin thinking about daily cleaning routines, start by clearing away your clutter. If you have magazines that need to be read, letters that should be answered, drawers and closets that could be better organized, clutter is part of your life and you need to deal with it. Banishing mess will make you feel more in control and less bogged down by chores. The more organized your home, the less daunting a task it will be to keep it clean.

TACKLING THE CLUTTER

Start by identifying the areas in your house that need work – this could be an entire room or a particular area, such as a cupboard or drawer. The next stage is to find seven large bags or boxes and a garbage sack, then mark and fill your bags and boxes as follows:

'Put away' Any items that have a designated home and need to be put away.
'Create a place' Items that you want to keep but currently have no place for.
'Action' Articles to read, letters to answer and so on.
'Repair' Anything that needs to be altered, repaired or cleaned before storing.
'Pass on' Items to donate to a charity.
'Recycle' Items such as glass, paper and clothing that you no longer need.
'Not sure' Any items that you cannot decide about.
'Rubbish/trash' Throw it away.

Write on each box or bag a deadline by which you intend to have the items in the container sorted out. If you regularly have clutter to deal with, you could create a permanent place to keep pending clutter. But to stop the contents from building up, schedule a regular time to sort it out – perhaps 30 minutes a week or an evening once a month.

This may seem like a lot of hard work, but once you have cleared the clutter from your home, it will feel fresh and revitalized and so will you. Once you can see the floor and the countertops, you will be in a better frame of mind for tackling the everyday tasks of cleaning, cooking and laundering. And a better organized life will give you time to do the things you really enjoy.

KEEPING ON TOP OF CLUTTER

All items that have found their way into your home should have a place to live. If they haven't, get hold of some easily accessible storage such as accordion files, drawers and boxes, and put things away. There should also be places for in-between items – clothes that you have worn and plan to wear again soon or magazines that are half read, for instance. If everything has somewhere to go, there is no excuse for it to be hanging around.

Get into the habit of putting things away as soon as you have finished with them – for example, when your clean washing is dry, put it in the drawers or closet immediately; when you have finished looking at a book, put it back on the shelf. Allocate yourself regular 'mail and paperwork time' so you can keep on top of your correspondence and make sure your paperwork is organized and filed.

Housekeeping: short, sweet and simple

In order to keep your housework under control, you need to create a system that works. This means building a routine that makes sense for you, your home and the people with whom you share it. The demands of a large house will not be the same as those of a studio apartment; and the home of a full-time working couple will not need the same upkeep as a house occupied by a family with two children and a dog. You may have hours to spend each day on keeping your home clean and tidy, or you may only have a few hours during your busy working week. Whatever your lifestyle, however, the housework basics are the same.

ESSENTIAL DAILY TASKS

If you don't have time to do the more arduous jobs around the home, simplify your routine as much as possible by doing only the essential daily tasks. This entails keeping the kitchen, bathroom(s), and bedroom(s) cleaned, not only for hygienic reasons, but also to keep you feeling in control of your home.

Bathroom

Clean surfaces and taps/faucets with a cloth soaked in a disinfectant bathroom cleaner or multi-surface spray. To avoid the build-up of scum, wipe down the shower cubicle or bathtub with a sponge or cloth after each use. Spraying shower cubicles with a special shower spray will prevent the build-up of mineral deposits. Hang wet towels to dry, but if they are sopping wet, change them. Your facecloth may need to be changed daily for hygienic purposes.

Bedroom

Make the beds first thing in the morning, but try to air them for a while first. Ventilate the bedrooms for at least half an hour every day, if you can.

Kitchen

Keep the kitchen clean, all dishes washed and pantry well stocked at all times. Clean up pots and pans as you work or stack them in the dishwasher. Even if you haven't got a full load, run a rinse cycle to prevent food from crusting over, or rinse them under the tap/faucet. Put out clean kitchen cloths and cleaning utensils every day.

Floors

Clean the floors in high-use areas, such as the kitchen and hallway/entryway, especially if you have pets or small children. Sweep, damp mop, or vacuum, as necessary.

Foods

Always keep some fresh vegetables and fruit available for a quick, healthy meal. Also keep on hand cooked chicken, cheese, ham or canned tuna, which can be added to a fresh salad for an instant dinner when time is short.

General cleaning

Although a maid service can be expensive, if you can't afford household help once a week, try to arrange to share one with a friend. Choose the most arduous tasks for the professional to do, such as cleaning windows or the inside of the oven.

Laundry

Try to do a little bit of laundry, whether it's washing, drying or ironing, twice a week, before it becomes an overwhelming chore. If cost-efficiency is your top priority, wait until you have a full load before washing.

Rubbish/trash

Empty rubbish and garbage containers from around the house at the end of every day, as a matter of hygiene.

> **Helpful hint:**
> Resist the urge to 'slack off,' even for just one day. The results of procrastination are worse than doing what needs to be done in the moment.

WEEKLY TASKS

Each of these jobs should be tackled at least once a week, some of them more often. Try to establish a weekly routine for these chores so you have a clear idea of what needs to be done on which day.

- Change bed linens.
- Toss pillows into a hot dryer for 15 minutes to freshen and eliminate mites.
- Change bath towels twice a week.
- Vacuum carpets and rugs twice a week; floors, upholstered furniture and lampshades weekly.
- Wash all hard-surface floors, such as stone, marble and slate, using a commercial cleaner.
- Dust all surfaces and objects that can be dusted, including pictures (don't forget the tops), mirrors, light fixtures and light bulbs.
- Wipe all fingerprints or smears from doorknobs, woodwork, telephones and computer keyboards. Use a soft cloth and anti-bacterial or disinfectant spray.
- Wash the entire bathroom: toilet, sink, wall tiles, toothbrush holders and all fixtures, cabinets and floor.
- Clean entire kitchen: clean refrigerator; wipe off stove (oven and burners) and other appliances inside and out; clean sinks, counter- and tabletops; wash splashbacks and scrub floors.
- Clean the oven linings if they are washable – catalytic linings shouldn't be scrubbed. You may need to clean the interior more often, depending on usage.
- Wash out and sanitize rubbish bins/garbage cans. Germs can, and do, accumulate there.
- Do food shopping once a week. If you keep an up-to-date market list, this should be easy. Set aside time on one day of the week as your shopping day. Keep a running list of what you need for the next meals and what you've run out of. Pick up extra items on interim shopping days: for instance, a certain day for the fish market and another for your farmer's market (if you have one), and neighbourhood store for forgotten items.
- Miscellaneous jobs: for example, cleaning out a utility drawer, going through old cosmetics, throwing out medicines that have expired and so on.

MONTHLY TASKS

Some of these jobs will need to be handled once a month, others slightly less frequently.

- Wash mirrors and glass panels at least once a month.
- Launder all bed linens including mattress covers, blankets, pillow covers, quilts and duvets/comforters at least every 3 months.
- Turn most frequently used mattresses every 4–6 months – flip from bottom to top as well as from side to side. You will need help with this.
- Vacuum the mattresses when you flip them.
- Launder pillows according to directions on labels/tags.
- Clean cooker/range-top hoods every 2–4 months.
- Wax or condition floors every 3–6 months.
- Go through drawers, cabinets and closets frequently to toss out what you no longer use and to clean out anything that's become sticky. Add moth-repellent strips or moth cakes to clothes drawers and closets. A good habit is to tackle one drawer or cabinet every week in rotation, particularly in the kitchen and bathroom, until they are all perfectly ordered.
- Clean and polish household metals at least every 3–6 months. Be careful to use the appropriate product for different metals: silver polish should not be used on brass or pewter and so on.

ANNUAL TASKS

These tasks will need to dealt with once every 6–12 months, depending on usage.

• Clean chandeliers, lamps and any other light fixtures once a year or more often if they are unusually dusty.

• Clean all wall surfaces, such as panelling and plaster, at least twice a year. You will probably need to remove finger smudges from walls more frequently than this. This can be done using a rag moistened with a solution made from 60 ml/¼ cup ammonia and 250 ml/1 cup water.

• Clean your storage areas once a year. Invest in good metal filing cabinets to store archival files and mementos. Get out of the habit of keeping old boxes that won't be used or looked in.

• Move all large appliances, such as the stove and refrigerator, and vacuum and damp-mop the area beneath and behind them at least once a year.

• Shampoo upholstery and carpeting (or call a professional service) every 1–2 years, depending on the area's usage. A carpeted bathroom or dining room will need shampooing at least once a year.

• Oil or condition skirting/baseboards every 6–12 months.

• Wash windows and screens a minimum of twice a year.

• Launder or dry-clean window treatments, such as drapes/ curtains, fabric blinds and Roman shades, every year.

• Go through your collection of books, CDs, videos and DVDs and dispose of what you no longer want; local charity/thrift shops or your public library will always have a use for them and give you a tax-deductible receipt. Keep ahead of this task by doing this once a year.

• Go through your clothes; if you haven't worn an item in 2 years, it's time for it to go. If you don't make room for the new, nothing new will come into your life. And if it does, you won't have a place for it.

Cleaning basics

In order to keep your home clean and sparkling, you need to have some basic cleaning tools and products. You will also need to know how to carry out basic techniques, such as dusting and mopping, to keep your house in tiptop condition. Before you start, make sure you have all the cleaning materials you need close by.

CLEANING PRODUCTS

Use cleaning products only on the surfaces and in the manner recommended on the label. Don't use a harsh cleanser when a mild all-purpose cleanser will do the job. When mixing solutions, add the water before the cleanser so you do not risk splashing the cleanser on surrounding surfaces. A concentrated cleanser is more effective diluted than straight out of the bottle. Always test a new product on a small area prior to using it all over.

To save time, put together a basic cleaning kit (*see* left) composed of products you need to clean the kitchen and the rest of the house. Keep this kit in a caddy organizer in an easy-to-access place, such as under the kitchen counter, so you know exactly where to find it when you need it. Every home is different. Go from room to room in your own home, making a list of everything you are going to need. It's a good idea to have a discreet cleaning kit in areas of high use such as the kitchen, the bathroom and the laundry room.

HOMEMADE CLEANSERS

In addition to knowing which cleaning products you need for each room and surface in your home, it's a good idea to be able to create your own cleaning solutions from common household ingredients. The following all-purpose disinfectant cleansers are generally safe to use on most surfaces.

Mild all-purpose cleanser
• Add 4 tablespoons bicarbonate of soda/baking soda to 1 litre/quart warm water. Mix well.
• Wipe the surface or structure, then rinse carefully.

Concentrated all-purpose cleanser
Do not use these solutions on aluminium, marble, crystal or porcelain.
• Mix 1 tablespoon each of ammonia and liquid laundry detergent in 500 ml/ 1 pint water and stir well.
• Alternatively, add 125 ml/½ cup bicarbonate of soda/baking soda to 4 litres/1 gallon warm water.

Semi-abrasive cleanser
Removes difficult stains on various surfaces in your home.
• Make a thick paste with bicarbonate of soda/baking soda and water.

Window cleaner
• Fill a spray bottle nearly to the top with half water and half rubbing alcohol. Top up with a little ammonia and mix.
• Spray on the window, then wipe with a dry, lint-free cloth.

Detergent solution
This solution is excellent for cleaning grease or water-soluble stains that appear on most surfaces.

• Mix 1 teaspoon clear washing-up liquid or detergent powder (containing no bleaches or strong alkalis) with 250 ml/1 cup warm (not hot) water.
• Dampen a white cloth in this solution and carefully rub out the stain until it is gone. Rinse well with clear water.

Ammonia solution
This is a highly effective solution used in cleaning stubborn floor stains, as well as kitchen appliances and painted wall surfaces. But caution should be used when applying to marble.
• Mix 1 tablespoon clear household ammonia with 125 ml/½ cup water.
• Dampen a white cloth in the solution and carefully rub the stain until it is gone. Once it has gone, neutralize the area with a vinegar solution (below) to avoid any possible skin irritation.

Vinegar solution
Used on glass, mirrors, laminates and chrome, vinegar is an excellent disinfectant and cleaner.
• Mix 1 part white vinegar with 2 parts water and apply with a cloth.

CAUTIONS

Do not mix chlorine bleach with acids, alkalis, ammonia or any substances that contain them.

Do not mix more solution than you intend to use in the near future, as it can lose efficacy over time.

When using chlorine bleach as a sanitizer, mix it fresh.

Store toxic and flammable materials in carefully, clearly and accurately labelled containers in a safe place, out of the reach of children. Never use food containers.

Follow all safety instructions on labels.

Make sure you have adequate ventilation when mixing toxic, flammable or strong-smelling substances.

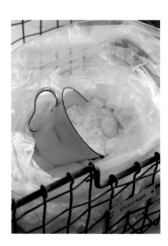

DUSTING

When you dust, start at the top of the house and work your way down. Do one room completely – seeing a newly dusted room will be a great incentive to move on to the next one.

Wood furniture

• Dust tops of wooden tables at least every other day. Thoroughly dust once a week.

• For all wood furniture, choose a soft, cotton rag – old cotton t-shirts are great for this – synthetic material won't absorb cleaning fluids, you need 100 per cent cotton.

• The simplest way to dust is to moisten – but not saturate – a cotton cloth with clear water, but this doesn't condition the wood in any way.

• Dust-removing sprays or cloths can be used on wooden surfaces, but avoid oils, which draw more dust and prints.

• Dust using a circular motion.

• Make sure to dust under lamps and knick-knacks.

• Dust intricate furnishings, such as those with carvings, with a small, soft brush, such as a natural-hair artist's brush or dry soft toothbrush.

• Clean all cloths and brushes when you are finished.

• Dusting mitts and furniture wipes, pre-treated with furniture polish, are available, which make the task even easier. Keep a box of them in your cleaning kit for ready access.

Glass-topped tables and monitors

• Dust glass-topped tables and television screens twice a week with a soft cloth and glass spray cleanser.

• Wipe down computer and television screens once a week. Check the manufacturer's instructions or retailer's recommendations for special cleaning pads for optical plastic and glass.

Ornaments, bibelots and knick-knacks

• Clean all objects twice a week.

• Dampen a soft cloth with water and a few drops of non-abrasive detergent, and clean porcelain or china figurines.

• Clean crystal objects with a glass spray cleanser.

• Dry dust all books with a soft rag or use the upholstery nozzle/tip of your vacuum cleaner to remove any dust settlements.

USING A BROOM

• Choose a broom with synthetic bristles for smooth indoor surfaces. Use a very stiff, tough broom for rougher outdoor areas. The best brooms are those that have an angled head.

• Starting at the far end of the room, gather the debris into a small pile.

• Sweep the pile into your dustpan and pour it into the dustbin/trash can.

• Any residue left on the floor can be picked up with a damp paper towel.

BASIC HOUSEHOLD CLEANING TOOLS

*A box, basket or bag
  for carrying kit*
Broom
Brushes
Bucket(s)
Cloths and rags
Dustpan with brush
Dust mop
Handheld vacuum
Mop – sponge or string
Plunger
*Vacuum cleaner with
  disposable bags,
  if necessary and
  attachments*

USING A MOP

These instructions are for wood floors and for everyday maintenance of tiled and stone floors. For details on how to clean other types of hard flooring, see pages 34–39.

• Mop your wood, tiled and hard floors at least once a week. Heavily soiled areas, such as the hallway/entryway, kitchen or bathroom, may need to be cleaned more often.
• Sweep the floor with a broom or anti-static cloth mop to remove as much dust as you can before you start the wet mopping process.
• Moisten your mop with clear water and an appropriate cleaner for the type of flooring. (Do not use soap on wood floors, but you can add a drop of wood-cleaning detergent to the water.)
• Rub the floor in a sweeping motion, forward and backward; do not make a circular motion.
• Lift the mop between strokes to avoid streaking the floor.
• Between strokes, shake off any dust that has gathered on the mop as you work. The mopping process will pick up any dust left behind by the broom.
• Choose a mop with a removable head that you can launder. String mops are best. Be sure to do so regularly, and use bleach in the water to disinfect it.

USING A VACUUM

• Keep carpets and rugs in top condition by regular vacuuming. Use doormats at the main entrances to your home to pick up soil from the street. Put castor cups/coasters under furniture to protect the carpets and rugs.
• Shampoo your carpets every 1–2 years, depending on whether you have children and pets.

• Use the floor attachment on your vacuum cleaner on bare floors or valuable carpets or rugs.
• For regular carpeting, use a power-brush attachment.
• To maintain beautiful wood floors, vacuum them along the grain of the wood.

SUCTION-SETTING GUIDELINES

High setting: *hard, bare floors, such as wood or tile, and carpets; grooves, indentations, seams and skirting/baseboards*
Medium setting: *valuable carpets*
Low setting: *draperies, upholstery, and throw rugs*

AREAS TO BE VACUUMED   VACUUM ATTACHMENTS

Areas to be vacuumed	Vacuum attachments
Cabinets, shelves and books	*All-purpose brush*
Difficult places to clean	*Crevice nozzle/tip*
Narrow areas, detailing	*Radiator brush*
Skirting/baseboards and moulding	*Dusting brush*
Upholstery	*Upholstery nozzle/tip*
Wood, stone, linoleum or vinyl floors	*Floor brush*

Bedroom basics

The bedroom is the one room in which you spend the most amount of time, though much of it is sleeping. This is where you recuperate, restore your energy levels and relax. In order to do this effectively, the room needs to be comfortable, welcoming, fresh and clean. Part of your daily schedule of 'living tidy' should include airing out the bed and bedroom. Replenishing your room's fresh air supply after a night's sleep is the healthiest routine you can instill into your housekeeping schedule.

BEDROOM ROUTINE

It takes very little time to get the bedroom straight in the morning. The daily tasks below should soon become an instinctive part of your routine.

Daily tasks

• Every morning, peel the bedclothes down to air out the bed. Leave this way for as long as you can: at least 1 hour if you are running off to work, but longer if you have more time. This will help to keep the bed fresh.

• Then make the bed, making sure to re-plump the pillows.

• Every morning, open the bedroom windows wide to let in fresh air. Keep them open for as long as possible. If you can leave the windows open all day, then do so.

• Put clothing away – dirty laundry in the laundry basket/hamper, clean clothing back in the wardrobe/closet.

• Put toiletries in their place.

• If a member of your family is ill, change their bed linen every day.

• Change baby linens daily.

Weekly tasks

• Straighten and dust each room at least once a week.

• Vacuum each bedroom twice a week, including the upholstery and window treatments, at least once a week.

• Change bed linens at least once a week.

• For anyone suffering from respiratory ailments, it is essential to launder all bed linen twice a week. Launder the linings (under-pillow cases and mattress covers) once a week.

• Toss all pillows into a hot dryer for 15 minutes once a week. This will kill dust mites, as well as freshen and fluff your pillows.

• If you can air your duvet/comforter, blankets and pillows/cushions outside in the fresh air, then do so. Sunshine not only kills dust mites, it will leave your bedding smelling fresh. Do this as often as is practical, but every 1–2 weeks is ideal.

Monthly tasks

• Change all bed linen, including mattress covers, blankets, pillow/cushion covers, duvets/comforters and quilts once a month. Do this more frequently if either you or your partner suffers from any respiratory ailments.

Yearly tasks

• Turn and flip all frequently used mattresses at least twice a year and vacuum them.

• If you have a yard or any outside space, air your mattress in the sunshine once or twice a year. This will keep it fresh.

Weekly schedule

Create and keep your own personal simple home calendar. Get into the habit of either writing out on a pad of paper or storing on a computer or tablet what needs to be done every day in your home. You will see that most of the time your daily and weekly chores fall into a set routine and do not deviate that much from week to week. The importance of setting your house-cleaning tasks into a written plan can't be stressed enough. Once you've completed a plan, you will be able to see ahead each day without panic and with the full confidence of knowing what you're doing, and the time it will take to do it. Having a clear picture in your mind of what needs to be done will allow you to complete the task with greater ease, and will eradicate the urge to slip into panic and disarray. Additionally, keeping on hand this simple home calendar is beneficial for anyone else who does the cleaning in your home. If you have outside help, it's so much simpler to hand them this completed schedule rather than needing to explain it over and over again. Simple for you; simple for them.

NOTES

	Morning	Afternoon	Evening
Monday			
Tuesday			
Wednesday			
Thursday			
Friday			
Saturday			
Sunday			

SPARKLING SURFACES

Walls, floors, carpets, windows, blinds, nooks and crannies – how you maintain these aspects of your home makes a world of difference! Let these surfaces go and your home will become dull and lifeless. Keep them gleaming and you and your guests will feel welcome the moment you step inside the door.

A safe home

Keeping the surfaces of your home spick and span will create a comfy retreat in which to live and relax. However, cleanliness is about more than simple aesthetics. Making sure floors and surfaces are germ-free is important in any home, but especially so if you have young children who are able to crawl. Also, if you have pets, floors and other surfaces will become dirty more quickly and your cleaning routine will need to take this into account. There are many household disinfectants that are effective against a wide variety of micro-organisms, but you can quite easily create your own cleaning solutions.

CLEANING BASICS

• Every surface in your home needs to be cleaned and maintained in a specific way, depending on the material it is made from, what it is used for, and how often it is used.

• Begin by making a list of all the surfaces in your home; then, carefully inventory the specific products needed for each of them.

• Have these cleaning products on hand. Keep a special utility cabinet located in an easy-to-access place for storing all your cleaning products and tools. Remember to keep caddies in each key room of your home!

• There are easily available, very basic essential products with which to clean every surface of your home. If you have all of the following products, they will be all you need to keep your whole home clean.

SURFACE CLEANING KIT

All-purpose cleanser for sinks, stainless steel, oven surfaces, etc.

Ammonia for glass, crystal, smudges on painted walls

Bicarbonate of soda/baking soda for the inside of the refrigerator

Bleach

Carpet spot cleaner

Ceramic tile cleaner

Chrome cleaner

Drain cleaner

Furniture polish

Spray glass cleaner

Hardwood floor cleaner

Heavy-duty cleanser for stubborn spots on sinks, etc.

Heavy-duty lubricant and cleanser for stubborn spots

Mild washing-up liquid/ dishwashing detergent

Oven cleaner

Silver polish

Stainless steel cleaner

Stone cleaner

Toilet-bowl cleaner

White vinegar for cleaning chrome taps/faucets, shower sets, and disinfecting

Deodorizing and disinfecting

Certain things in the home, such as countertops, floors, personal hygiene items, flowerpots and vases need particular care in deodorizing and disinfecting. These need to be done weekly.

Floors and countertops: vinyl, linoleum, ceramic tile
• Mop or wipe with a solution comprised of 125 ml/½ cup bleach per 4 litres/ 1 gallon warm water.
• Keep the floor or countertop wet for at least 5 minutes.
• Rinse with clear water and let air dry.

Hairbrushes and combs
• Make a solution from 1 teaspoon bleach to ½ litre/quart warm water.
• Immerse the brush or comb in the solution for 5 minutes.
• Rinse with clear water. Stand the brush on its bristles and let air dry.

Flowerpots and planters
• Wash thoroughly with soapy/sudsy water and rinse.
• Then make a cleaning solution from 125 ml/½ cup bleach and 4 litres/ 1 gallon water.
• Immerse the pots in the solution and let soak for 5 minutes, then rinse in clear water.

Cut flowers
• Add a few drops of bleach to each 1 litre/quart of cold water in the flower vase. This solution will keep your flowers fresh by killing bacteria that would otherwise rot them. It will also clean and deodourize vases (except cut crystal) and remove stains and odors.
• When the cut flowers have finished blooming, wash the vase with warm, soapy/sudsy water, then rinse well.

• To thoroughly clean vases, fill them with a solution of 125 ml/½ cup bleach per 4 litres/1 gallon water and let stand for 5 minutes. Rinse well.

Litter boxes and plastic animal cages
• Empty all the old litter into the dustbin/garbage can.
• Wash and scrub the litter box or cage in the sink using scalding, soapy/sudsy water. Make sure you wear rubber gloves used only for this purpose to protect your hands.
• Rinse well.
• Disinfect the box by filling with a solution of 60 ml/¼ cup bleach and 4 litres/1 gallon hot water. Let stand for 10 minutes. Gently swish the water around the sides of the box.
• Rinse thoroughly, then let air dry.
• Refill with fresh litter or bedding.

HOMEMADE DISINFECTANTS AND SANITIZERS

Many ingredients found in chemists, drugstores and hardware stores make effective disinfectants and sanitizers. But if you want to make your own solutions, follow these instructions.

Chlorine bleach

Chlorine bleach is a ready-made solution that you can purchase at most grocery stores and supermarkets, or you can make your own. To do so, add 150 ml/¾ cup bleach to 4 litres/1 gallon warm water. Wash the surface or object with a clean cloth dipped in the solution. Keep the surface wet with the solution for 10 minutes. Rinse with clear water and let air dry.

It is an excellent all-purpose cleansing solution to have in your home, and can be used for the following purposes:

• To sanitize, sterilize, disinfect, clean and deodorize.
• To combat a wide range of bacteria, viruses and moulds.
• To bleach and sanitize laundry.
• To deodorize and whiten cloth nappies/diapers.
• To disinfect and deodorize kitchen cloths.

Alcohol

A solution of alcohol and water sterilizes and evaporates immediately, leaving a clear, clean surface. Apply a small amount of the solution to a clean cloth and wipe dry. Do not use on laminated glass, wood surfaces or laminates, as alcohol will dull them. Test on an inconspicuous area of other surfaces before using. This advice also applies to window and glass cleaners containing ammonia.

Ethyl alcohol or ethanol Used for antiseptic purposes to clean bathroom fixtures. It is an excellent cleanser for glass and crystal; use a solution of 1 part water with 1 part ethyl alcohol. Much more expensive than isopropyl alcohol, it is nevertheless interchangeable with it in use.

Isopropyl alcohol or rubbing alcohol Used for antiseptic purposes to clean bathroom fixtures. You may mix it with water to clean crystal, use 1 part water with 1 part isopropyl alcohol. This is less expensive and more readily available than ethanol alcohol.

HOMEMADE CHLORINE BLEACH

This homemade solution (see left) can be used on the following items and surfaces:

Baby furniture
Bathtubs
Bidets
Nappy bins/diaper pails
Enamel-painted surfaces
Fibreglass
Household bins/trash cans
Latex-painted surfaces
Plastic items and surfaces
Plasticized baby bedding
Refrigerators
Sinks and countertops
Toilets
Vitreous china

Never use this solution on the following surfaces:
Stone (including marble)
Upholstery
Wood

Pets in the home

Keeping pets in your home is both enjoyable and rewarding. Animals are adored by children and adults alike, and they can make wonderful companions for people who live on their own. Having a pet in the home does have its drawbacks, however. Muddy paws and pet hairs will have an impact on the amount and regularity of cleaning, and this will have to be taken into account when planning your housekeeping routine.

ESSENTIAL TASKS

When you share your home with a pet, there are daily and weekly tasks that need to be carried out. Clean out litter boxes daily and change them weekly. Wash your pet's bedding at least once a week. Vacuum or wash floors on a weekly basis. Use a disinfectant solution on hard floors.

Pet rules

1. Wash your hands after petting, handling or grooming the pet and before eating.
2. Keep cats and other pets off countertops and tables.
3. Do not let pets eat off the same plates or drink from the same water glasses as the family, and wash pet dishes separately from those of the family. Keep special water and food dishes for pets, and keep them scrupulously clean. Do not simply refill them with food day after day, but wash them in hot, soapy/sudsy water after each use.
4. Do not let pets beg at the table or take food from anyone's hand during a meal. Be careful that pets do not eat your baby's or toddler's food. Little ones sometimes enjoy this, but it is a bad habit for the pets and the children to get into.
5. Do not feed pets raw or undercooked food. You can give them or, indirectly, a member of the family a food-borne illness.
6. Do not let pets sleep on the beds. Be particularly careful with children's beds and furniture.
7. Do not let dogs sit on your furniture. Dogs can be trained to stay on the floor and should be provided with a soft, comfortable bed of their own.

HOUSEKEEPING PROBLEMS WITH CATS AND DOGS

Our furry friends give us companionship and welcome us home. We need to take care of them to prevent problems such as poor behaviour and an unhygienic environment.

Clawing furniture and unruly behaviour

• Keep a cat's claws trimmed.
• Train the cat to scratch the scratching post and not your furniture.
• Choose upholstery that does not snag cat's claws.
• Invest in 'soft paws' (little plastic covers glued over claws to prevent damage).
• Invest in obedience training for dogs that chew furniture.
• Get chew toys to keep your pet occupied and dog-repelling sprays for use on furniture.

Litter boxes

• Change cat litter as soon as you detect any odour – or once a week, regardless.
• Litter that can be 'scooped' does not require changing as often, and dust-resistant litter reduces odours and allergic reactions.
• Keep the litter box in a well-ventilated area, but not the kitchen or dining areas. The bathroom should also be avoided – it is generally not a well-ventilated area in most homes and would promote bacterial/viral growth.
• Sanitize, disinfect and deodorize the litter box at least twice a week (see page 30).

Food and water bowls

• Wash with warm soapy/sudsy water and rinse.
• Fill with a solution of 1 tablespoon bleach per 4 litres/1 gallon water.
• Let stand for 2 minutes. Drain, rinse well and let air dry.

Outdoor garbage cans

• Sanitize, disinfect and deodorize outdoor dustbins/garbage cans that contain pet droppings.
• First, empty and wash with warm soapy/sudsy water.
• Rinse thoroughly.
• Wash out with a solution of 125 ml/½ cup bleach per 4 litres/1 gallon water.
• Keep the surface wet for at least 5 minutes.
• Rinse and let air dry.

Ticks and fleas

• Wash your pet and comb his or her coat regularly. Alternatively, take to a pet-grooming service.
• Vacuuming gets rid of fleas, eggs, larvae and possibly ticks. So, if your pet has fleas, vacuum your house daily until the problem is cured. Throw away the vacuum bag every time you vacuum because the fleas will continue to live inside. Special sprays for carpets and household surfaces are available from your vetinary surgery or online.
• Most fleas and eggs will be in or near the pet's bed and bedding, so vacuum this area daily.
• If there are fleas, wash your pet's bedding more than once a week in hot, soapy/sudsy water. Rinse well.
• To avoid ticks, keep your lawn well mowed, cut back undergrowth/underbrush and weeds, and prevent pets from roaming during tick season (late spring and summer).
• If your pet gets ticks, wash him or her with a good tick and flea shampoo – ask your vet for a good brand.
• Put a flea collar on your pet, use anti-flea and anti-tick sprays, liquids and bombs, and repeat until the infestation is gone. If the infestation is bad, call a local or national pest-control service (see page 153 and 155) that will have details of companies in your area.
• You can prevent fleas and ticks altogether by using a pet medication that you dab on the pet's neck once a month. Ask your vet for a good brand. Alternatively, add oral medication to your pet's food.

Pet odours

• Brush and groom your pet once a week.
• Wash your pet once a month.
• Launder your pet's bedding weekly, especially his or her bedding or whatever he or she sleeps on.
• Vacuum your home at least once a week.
• Clean your pet's bed frequently.
• Change the litter box frequently and do so outdoors, if possible. Many litters now contain scent controls, but they should still be cleaned often.
• Keep litter boxes and cages out of living spaces and in well-ventilated areas.
• Ventilate your home thoroughly.
• Let your pet spend time outdoors, if possible.
• Shampoo carpets more frequently than might otherwise be necessary – at least twice a year – and, if your pets sit on the furniture, shampoo the upholstery regularly, too.

HARDWOOD FLOORS

Wood is a rich, lustrous choice for flooring. It's beautiful, easy to maintain and retains its functionality for many years. In some instances, it may be more expensive to buy than other flooring, but it will last a lifetime if given the proper care. Wood floors can be natural (untreated), stained, sealed, waxed and/or hard-finished. Natural floors require some degree of finishing to enhance and protect, while hard-finished floors provide a barrier between the wood and the world.

Stained and sealed wood floors

Hardwood floors can be stained to add colour and beauty while still showing the original grain. Sealants penetrate the wood and protect the finish from scratches.

Routine maintenance

• Remove loose dirt daily with a dust mop, broom or vacuum. If you are using a vacuum cleaner, a floor brush attachment does the best job, but is the most awkward option.
• Never leave a spill to settle; wipe it up at once. For quick clean-ups, use a dust mop or broom.
• Damp-mop every few days with an almost dry mop.
• Vacuum well once a week, making sure you go right into the corners of each room.
• On sealed floors, use a few drops of washing-up/dishwashing liquid or a gentle detergent and warm water to create a soapy/sudsy water solution. Alternatively, use a specialized wood floor cleaner, available from supermarkets or online. Avoid ammonia-based cleansers.
• Maintain with a specialized hardwood floor sealant (available from hardware and DIY stores) and dusters.
• Do not apply sprays or oils meant for wood furniture because they will make floors slippery and dangerous to walk on.

Helpful hint:
Be sure to catch, and deal with, any spot the minute it occurs on your floor, no matter what type of floor you have. If left, it may become harder to remove.

Floors

Floors in a house show off its essential character. No matter what surface you choose, whether it's hardwood, tile, stone or laminate, your floors reflect the soul of your home and its fundamental design. A floor provides the depth and expanse of a room, and as such, it should be kept clean, uncluttered, and gleaming. An understanding of how to clean and maintain each and every floor surface is imperative for a well-kept home.

Unsealed and waxed wood floors

Stained floors that are neither waxed nor sealed with urethane are not impervious to water, so all water spills must be wiped up to prevent surface damage. Avoid using water or water-based cleansers on unsealed wood floors.

Routine maintenance

• Treat stains immediately (see below).
• Lightly sand scratches smooth.
• Repair by applying wax.

Scratches and stains tips

Dark spots and ink stains Try the water spot treatment below. If the stain persists, apply household bleach or vinegar and leave it for up to 1 hour. Wipe with a moist cloth, then dry and finish with fine sandpaper. Stain, wax and hand-buff.

Gum and wax drippings Put a plastic bag filled with ice on the gum or wax until it is dry enough to remove. Carefully lift off with a dull-edged knife such as a spatula or palette knife. Put an ink blotter on candle wax or crayon and heat with an iron on the opposite side. It should lift once warm.

Heel scratches Work in a little floor wax with fine steel wool, then hand-buff.

Mould Rub with a specialized wood cleanser.

Oily stains Soak a cotton cloth with hydrogen peroxide and put it on the stain. Then soak another cloth with ammonia and lay on top of the first. Repeat until the stain is gone. Air dry, then hand-buff.

Organic stains Rub with a moist cloth. Start at the outside of the stain and work inward. Dry and wax.

Scratches and wear To avoid scratches, use protective felt pads under furniture legs and never drag heavy objects over the floor. Use a colour stick and floor wax to repair.

Water spots Rub spot with fine steel wool. If this doesn't work, gently rub with fine sandpaper and clean with fine steel wool and mineral spirits or a wood floor cleaner. Let dry. Stain, wax and hand-buff.

Waxy build-up Remove the old wax with odourless mineral spirits or a wood floor product made for stripping wax. Use rags and fine steel wool to strip any residue. When dry, wax again and hand-buff.

Hard-finished wood floors: urethane, polyurethane, varnish or shellac

Polyurethane finishes can be applied to hardwood flooring. They provide the wood with a coating which acts as a barrier to damage, protecting it from moisture and wear and tear. Because they suffer less damage, floors treated with polyurethane are the easiest to keep looking good.

Routine maintenance

• Vacuum or dust the floor thoroughly.
• Wash with warm, soapy/sudsy water. Use mild soap or a neutral pH detergent.
• Apply the mixture to your mop or cloth, not directly to the floor, and sweep over the floor.
• After washing the floor, rinse well.
• Shine with a buffing pad on a stick.
• Do not use a wax polish over a urethane finish, since wax does not adhere to urethane.
• Avoid strong or abrasive cleansers as they will harm the finish.
• Avoid oil-based cleansers, ammonia-based cleansers and alkaline cleansers.

Scratches and stains tips

If the scratches or stains are in the shellac only, the floor has probably been finished with a non-penetrating sealant. Repair with a touch-up kit made for urethane finishes, available from wood-flooring retailers or DIY stores.

Cigarette burns Most common burns can be treated with a touch-up kit made for urethane finishes. Rub with sandpaper, stain and refinish. For extreme burns, individual plank or parquet boards may need to be replaced.

Food, water, or dark spots Use a cleanser developed specifically for urethane finishes to remove the spot or stain. Resistant stains need extra work with the cleanser and a wood-flooring scrub pad made for urethane finishes.

Gum and wax drippings Put a plastic bag filled with ice on the wax until it is dry enough to remove. Clean the stain with a product for urethane finishes.

Oily spots Rub the spot with a cleanser developed for urethane finishes.

STONE FLOORS

Porous stone absorbs stains, cracks easily and can streak and scuff. The harder the stone, the less likely it is to scratch.

Polished stone floors

Granite or limestone have a medium-high gloss, and are suitable for bathrooms and kitchens. Their sealed surfaces make it impenetrable to oils and it is easily cleaned.

Honed stone floors

Honed limestone and granite have an even finish and are not glossy. They should be used in areas where there is a lot of traffic, but not in a kitchen, as they can be porous and cooking oils can easily penetrate the surface.

Flamed finish stone floors

Granite floor tiles and ceramic tiles can be flame finished which gives a rough texture and is an excellent choice for the kitchen, outdoor patio, or any high-traffic area.

Highly-glossed stone floors

Marble needs the most maintenance. Every little scratch or nick will show, so this type of surface should only be used in areas that get little traffic. Avoid spilling any alcohol-based products, such as wine or cleaning products, which etch marble.

Routine maintenance

A simple regime of regular dusting or vacuuming and washing with a neutral detergent should be all that is required. The use of specialized cleansers, sealants and waxes is unnecessary for the maintenance of stone floors.

- Vacuum once or twice a week to keep the floors looking good.
- Clean stone floors weekly. Use a mop, soft sponge, cloth or bristled scrub brush, with water mixed with a neutral pH detergent.
- Rinse thoroughly with a damp mop, then dry with soft cloths.
- Never use abrasive or caustic cleaning products.
- Don't use soap to clean stone floors because it may leave a film. All stone is best maintained with a neutral cleanser.
- Contact a professional floor cleaner for serious stain removal.
- Polishing and resealing should take place every 2½–3 years and should be carried out by a professional service.

SPOT REMOVAL BASICS

There are specific ways of dealing with spots and stains on most types of stone floors. Remember, the quicker you get to the stain, the easier it will be to remove it effectively.

Blot the spill at once with a white cloth. Never wipe the spill or it will spread.

Soak the stain with water and a mild detergent.

Rinse thoroughly with clear water. Dry with a clean, dry cloth.

Repeat the process if the stain persists.

MARBLE FLOORS

Marble is a stone that requires special care. It absorbs stains and will etch from acid spills or alcohol-based products, such as wine or cleaning products. Mop up any spills at once. Marble should not be used in high-traffic areas, such as the kitchen, but is highly suitable and beautiful when used in bathrooms. Water should be wiped up immediately, because it will leave a mark. Regular maintenance should include yearly deep-cleaning and buffing by a professional stone and marble polisher.

Routine maintenance
• Sweep or vacuum up dirt and soil particles regularly.
• Clean at least once a week with a neutral pH soap or a few drops of mild washing-up/dishwashing liquid and warm water.
• Wipe up any spills with a clean, soft cloth.
• Rinse floors and dry with a clean cloth.
• Apply a sealant/sealer, available at tile retailers, stone dealers and DIY stores, to floors every 2 years to prevent deep stains.
• Do not use abrasive cleansers, which can scratch the surface.
• Do not use vinegar or lemon-based cleansers, which can etch the surface.
• Polishing and resealing should take place every 2½–3 years by a professional service.
• It is not advisable to use penetrating sealants/sealers on marble floors.

Stain removal
• Use a ready-made poultice, available at tile retailers, stone dealers and DIY stores to remove stains.
• Do not use acids or abrasives, such as vinegar or scouring powders.
• It is recommended that you use ammonia only when absolutely necessary.
• Use stone and marble polishes to remove water rings, minor scratches or dull spots.
• Mild abrasives should only be used sparingly. Follow the manufacturer's directions and proceed with caution.
• Contact a stone dealer for serious stain removal.

GRANITE FLOORS

Granite is extremely tough and stain-proof, and is excellent for use in the kitchen or high usage areas. It is easy to clean and impervious to stains, burns and nicks. It keeps its lustre for a long time.

Routine maintenance
• Sweep or vacuum up dirt and soil particles regularly.
• Clean as needed with a neutral pH soap or a few drops of mild washing-up/dishwashing liquid and warm water. Wash with a soft sponge.
• Avoid abrasive cleansers, which can scratch. Also avoid ammonia and non-chlorine bleach.
• Rinse with a clean, soft cloth.
• Polishing and resealing should take place every 2½–3 years by a professional service.

Stain removal
• First, scrape off as much of the stain as possible.
• Use a ready-made poultice, available at tile retailers, stone dealers and DIY stores to remove the stain.
• For difficult organic stains, use a solution of 1 part water to 1 part chlorine bleach sparingly.
• Brush the solution on and leave until the stain disappears. Rinse with clear water.
• Contact a stone dealer for serious stain removal.

LIMESTONE FLOORS

Limestone absorbs stains and will etch from acid spills, so it's not a good choice for a kitchen floor – unless it is heavily sealed – as splashes from oils can penetrate the surface. However, limestone is highly suitable for other common areas of your home, such as a hallway/entryway or living room.

Routine maintenance
• Sweep or vacuum up dirt and soil particles regularly.
• Mop up any spills at once.
• Mop weekly with a few drops of washing-up/dishwashing liquid and warm water. Rinse with clear water and dry with a clean cloth.
• Apply a sealant/sealer, available at tile retailers and DIY stores, to floors every 2 years to prevent deep stains.
• Don't use abrasive cleansers, which can scratch, or vinegar or lemon-based cleansers, which can etch.
• Polishing and resealing should take place every 2½–3 years by a professional service.

Stain removal
• Use a ready-made poultice, available at tile retailers, stone dealers and DIY stores, to remove any stains.
• Contact a professional cleaner for serious stain removal.

SLATE FLOORS

Slate is a very rugged stone, which looks great as floor tiles. It is a hard, non-porous stone, which is perfect for use in kitchens and hallways/entryways. It requires very little daily maintenance, and retains its beauty for a long time, provided it is resealed and buffed by a professional on a regular basis.

Routine maintenance
• Sweep or vacuum up dirt and soil particles regularly.
• Clean at least once a week with a neutral pH soap or washing-up/dishwashing liquid and warm water.
• Rinse with clear water and dry well with a clean cloth.
• Apply a penetrating sealant/sealer, available at stone dealers and DIY stores, to floors every 2 years to prevent deep stains.
• Do not use abrasive cleansers, vinegar or lemon-based cleansers, which can etch.
• Polishing and resealing should take place every 2½–3 years by a professional service.

Stain removal
• To remove soap scum, clean with solution made from 125 ml/½ cup ammonia to 4 litres/1 gallon water.
• Contact a stone dealer for serious stain removal.

SPOT-REMOVAL CHART FOR STONE FLOORS

Efflorescence
Sometimes water brings minerals to the surface, which causes a flower-like powder stain to spread on stone. Vacuum or dust off.

Etch marks
Clean with water. Spread marble-polishing powder. Shine well with clean white cloth until etch is gone.

Fire and burn marks
Use a specialized 'smoke remover.'

Ink
For light-coloured stone, use bleach or hydrogen peroxide. For dark-coloured stone, use acetone.

Oil-based
(cooking oil, grease, tar, cosmetics)
Rub with a solution made from a liquid cleanser and ammonia, or bleach or mineral spirits. Never mix bleach and ammonia! Dangerous fumes can result.

Organic
(blood, urine, fruit, tobacco, coffee, tea, food, grass, animal droppings)
Rub with a mixture made up of 12 per cent hydrogen peroxide and ½ teaspoon ammonia.

Metal
Remove with a ready-made poultice.

Paint
Remove small amounts with lacquer thinner or scrape off carefully. Use commercial 'heavy liquid' stripper for heavy coverage.

Parasitic growths
(algae, mildew, lichen, moss, fungi)
Treat with ammonia, bleach or hydrogen peroxide: make up a solution of 125 ml/ ½ cup to 4 litres/1 gallon water.

Scratches and nicks
Rub with dry, fine steel wool. Cracks should be refinished by a stone repolishing service.

Water damage
Buff with dry, fine steel wool.

CARPETED FLOORS

To prolong the life of your carpets, it is important to vacuum them regularly. Thorough vacuuming at least once a week, and more often in heavy traffic areas, will remove dirt particles before they become embedded in the pile. Shampoo your carpets from time to time. For best results, get your carpet professionally cleaned.

Spot prevention

• To prevent dirt from the outside getting onto your carpet, put absorbent mats at each entrance to your home. Shake the mats outside and away from where people walk to prevent the dust from being brought back in.

• Change filters in your heating and air-conditioning systems every 6 months to prevent stains from forming around the vents.

• Clean traffic lanes periodically with an absorbent powder. Keep absorbent cloths or paper towels and cleaning solutions on hand for quick response to spills and accidents.

• Do not apply stain-repellent treatments that contain silicone, because they tend to accelerate carpet soiling.

Spot removal basics

• Whenever anything is dropped or spilled, remove as much of the spill as you can as quickly as possible using absorbent cloths or paper towels. Always have the necessary cleaning material to hand.

• Always work inward from the edge of the spill to prevent spreading it.

• Do not rub a spill – it may cause the spot to spread or distort the pile.

• Blot up liquid spills with an absorbent white towel or thick paper towel. Do not rub. For a liquid spill, pour sparkling/soda water or seltzer sparingly over the area; the bubbles will cause more of the spilled substance to rise to the surface, which should then be blotted quickly.

• Scoop up solid spills with a spoon or the end of a blunt-edged knife.

• Once the spill is removed, most spots can be dealt with effectively, using the foam from the suds of a solution of water and a mild detergent. Otherwise, use the relevant spot-removal agent (see opposite).

• For a wool carpet, or any wool blend, use products which specify 'Suitable for use on wool carpets.'

• Never drench or soak the carpet. After cleaning, blot as dry as possible with thick paper towels.

• Remove any remaining stain with carpet shampoo or commercial stain removers, following the manufacturer's instructions.

• Finally, rinse with clear, warm water, either by spraying the water onto the carpet, taking care not to get it too wet, or by patting it on with a clean white cloth or thick paper towel. Then blot thoroughly to dry.

• Once dry, brush the pile back to normal with the brush attachment of your vacuum cleaner, or a whisk broom.

• To raise the pile of a crushed carpet, cover the area with a damp cloth and hold a hot iron over the cloth. Brush up to lift pile when dry.

CARPET SPOT-REMOVAL CHART

Apply the spot-removal agent to a clean towel or cloth, not directly to the spot. Use small quantities at a time.

ORDER OF TREATMENT

ITEM	Step 1	Step 2	Step 3
Alcoholic beverages	1	2	~~
Bleach*	1	3	~~
Blood	1	2	13
Butter	4	2	~~
Candlewax	5	14	9
Chewing gum	5	4	~~
Chocolate	2	3	6
Coffee	1	2	4
Colas and soft drinks	1	2	~~
Cooking oils	4	2	~~
Cream	2	4	~~
Egg	4	2	~~
Floor wax	4	2	~~
Fruit juice	1	2	9
Furniture polish	4	2	3
Gravy and sauces	7	2	~~
Ink (fountain pen)	1	2	~~
Ink (ballpoint)	4	9	2
Ink (felt tip)	7	2	8
Ketchup	7	2	~~
Lipstick	4	2	~~
Milk	7	4	2
Mustard	2	~~	~~
Nail polish	8	4	2
Oil and grease	4	2	~~
Paint (latex)	1	2	4
Paint (oil)*	9	4	13
Rust	4	2	10
Salad dressing	2	4	~~
Shoe polish	4	2	~~
Soot	4	2	3
Tar	4	~~	~~
Tea	1	2	4
Urine (fresh)	1	2	~~
Urine (old)	2	3	6
Vomit	2	~~	~~
Wine	1	2	~~
Unknown material	4	12	2

* Unlikely to be removed

CLEANING AGENT

1. Soda water or cold tap water
2. Detergent solution or carpet-shampoo solution
3. Ammonia solution
4. Solvent
5. Chill with aerosol freezing agent or ice cubes in plastic bag. Pick or scrape off
6. Vinegar solution
7. Warm water
8. Clear nail-polish remover (preferably acetone)
9. Alcohol or mineral spirits, turpentine
10. Rust remover
11. Absorbent powder (for example, salt or talc)
12. Commercial absorbent cleaner
13. Professional cleaning
14. Absorbent paper and iron

Helpful hint:
Damp-mop all painted skirting boards/baseboards and trim at least once a month to remove dirt and debris. Your walls will look dingy if you don't!

OTHER FLOOR SURFACES

Besides the usual surfaces already discussed, there are other floors you can choose. Some of the hardiest are vinyl, linoleum and cork. Familiarize yourself with all the floor surfaces in your house and the particular ways to maintain their beauty.

Glazed ceramic and glass tiles

Caring for your ceramic and glass tiles is simple. Weekly maintenance of your tiled floor makes the difference between a glowing, sparkling room and one that is drab.

Routine maintenance

• For ceramic tiles, wash with any mild cleanser and soft sponge or cloth. Be sure that the cleanser is non-abrasive, non-acidic and doesn't contain ammonia.
• For glass tiles, use a commercial glass tile spray cleaner. For calcium deposits, use a specific cleanser indicated for this use.

Grout

Grout contains acrylic and has been treated with a penetrating sealant/sealers created to protect all medium-to-dense porous surfaces. Even with this protection, grout can become dingy. Establish a monthly routine for cleaning it, just as you would the surrounding surface.

Routine maintenance

• If your tiled floor is in the bathroom, weekly cleaning is recommended to prevent soap-scum build-up on the grout. The best cleaning tool to use is an old toothbrush.
• If there is soap-scum build-up or mildew on the grout, then use a specialized cleaning product or a toothbrush dipped in a bleach solution. Always test on a small area first and follow the manufacturer's instructions; try not to get the product on the ceramic tile finish.
• Do not use abrasive cleansers.

Painted floorboards, skirting boards/baseboards and trim

Painted floorboards, skirting boards/baseboards and trim can be cleaned with a damp mop. If your floor is carpeted, clean your skirting boards/baseboards and trim with a damp cloth. Because of the tread, floorboards may gather dust and grime in hidden places so take extra care when cleaning them.

Routine maintenance

• Clean once a month.
• Spray static-proof furniture polish on your mop or cloth after damp-mopping, then wipe it over the boards. Or, use a cloth treated with furniture polish.
• Wax once a year.

Laminate

Laminates are usually made from a wood composite base with a laminate surface that has been treated with an acrylic topcoat for greater durability. It is highly impervious to dirt and grime and easy to care for, but it will scratch. It is excellent for use in playrooms or home offices.

Routine maintenance

• Sweep or vacuum up dirt and soil particles regularly.
• Clean weekly with a recommended cleanser. Alternatively, use a cleansing solution made from 125 ml/½ cup vinegar per 4 litres/1 gallon water.
• Do not use soap-based detergents, abrasive cleansers, mop-and-shine products or paste wax, all of which leave a dull film on the surface.
• Contact a floor retailer for serious stain removal and repolishing.

Stain removal

• For tough stains, rub scuff marks with a nylon pad, sponge or soft nylon brush. Remove shoe polish with an acetone-based nail-polish remover.

Vinyl

Vinyl is a plastic and can be cleaned with a mild solution of water and vinegar. It is very hard-wearing and comes in a variety of colours and patterns. It is excellent for use in playrooms, kitchens and bathrooms. It is easy to maintain, takes a lot of abuse and will retain its character, provided it is cleaned regularly.

Routine maintenance

• Sweep or vacuum up dirt and soil particles regularly.
• Mop at least once a week with a neutral pH soap and warm water.

Alternatively, make a cleansing solution from 125 ml/½ cup ammonia per 4 litres/1 gallon water.
• Do not use abrasive cleansers.
• Polishing and resealing should take place every 2–3 years by a professional service.

Stain removal

• For tough stains, rub scuff marks with a nylon pad, sponge or soft nylon brush dipped in an ammonia solution or isopropyl alcohol. Rinse well.

Linoleum

Also known as 'vinyl sheet flooring', linoleum is a resilient floor made of cork, limestone, wood flour, linseed oil and resin, backed with jute. It will take a lot of wear and is easy to clean, ideal for bathroom floors.

Routine maintenance

• Sweep with a dust mop or broom.
• Do not use abrasive cleansers.
• Wash with soapy/sudsy water and a sponge mop.
• Rinse with clear water and buff dry.
• You can wax with paste or liquid wax.
• Contact a retailer for serious stain removal.
• Polishing and resealing should take place every 2–3 years by a professional service.

Cork

Cork flooring is excellent for playrooms and living areas. It is a warm, quiet flooring, best used in areas not exposed to a lot of strong sunlight. Usually installed as a floor tile and sealed with urethane, cork floors can easily be cleaned with a mop and a gentle cleanser.

Routine maintenance

• Sweep or vacuum up dirt and soil particles regularly.
• Mop weekly with a small amount of warm, soapy/sudsy water – the mop should never be more than just barely damp. Air dry.

Walls and ceilings

Cleaning of painted or wood surfaces should be factored into your maintenance schedule, even if it's only once every 6 months. It's important to keep dust, smudges, grime and dirt off walls or a home will start to look sad and shabby, and the rooms will seem perceptibly smaller. Clean walls also make for a healthier environment.

PAINTED SURFACES

There is nothing worse than pristine white walls displaying fingerprints from the your local newspaper! These can be removed simply by going over the area with a clean cloth dampened with a dab of ammonia and water. Keep your cleaning utensils handy in their caddy and remove these marks when you see them.

Routine maintenance

• Use the long brush attachment of your vacuum cleaner and work from ceiling to skirting boards/baseboards. Dust cloths and dry sponges will also work, but they take more effort. Do this with every change in season.
• Use a mild solution of soap and water to wipe away minor stains. Washing-up/dishwashing liquid is ideal.
• Mouldy ceilings should be scrubbed with a brush using a solution of 250 ml/1 cup chlorine bleach per 4 litres/ 1 gallon water. To prevent mould on the ceiling, use enamel paints containing anti-mildew agents.

Enamel paints, semi-gloss or glossy paints

These paints are washable and should be washed in the following way:
• Lay a drop cloth on the floor.
• Vacuum walls and ceilings.
• Set up a sturdy, stable ladder.
• Use a mild all-purpose detergent or household cleanser diluted in water. Test a small area first.
• Use a second pail of clean water for rinsing.
• Wash and rinse in small sections. Experts say to start at the bottom and move up (opposite direction may streak dirty water down a dry wall).

Latex paints

Latex paint is not washable, but for general touch-ups, do the following:
• Use a non-abrasive, mild cleanser and water with a cellulose sponge, not a cloth. Rinse with a damp sponge.
• If walls are very dirty, use a solution made from 2 tablespoons laundry detergent powder in 1 gallon warm (not hot) water.

Oil-based glazing

• Use a solution of water and ammonia on a clean cloth. Spot-rub gently.

Acrylic paint

• Put a small amount of ammonia on a clean damp cloth. Rub gently or the finish will come off.

WALLPAPER

Dusting is normally enough for regular maintenance. With the variety of textures and paper quality, look at the manufacturer's instructions for specific care.

Routine maintenance

• Dust with a clean cloth once a month.
• If the paper can be washed, damp-clean using warm, soapy/ sudsy water. Rinse thoroughly at once.
• Do not overwet: this will create buckling.
• Always test a small area of wallpaper with a cleaning solution first, to make sure there is no loss of colour or staining.
• Never use harsh cleansers or sponges.
• If the paper cannot be washed, use an India/art-gum rubber/eraser or stale bread dough rolled into balls.

Spot removal

• First, dust the wall.
• To remove scuff marks, ink and crayon, make a thick paste with water and bicarbonate of soda/baking soda. Test a spot first. Rub on the mark, then remove with a cloth.
• Dry-cleaning products may remove spots. Or use other commercial preparations.

WOODEN SURFACES

The beauty of wood warms the home. Regular care will enhance the richness of the colour and prevent the wood from drying out or experiencing other damage.

Panelling, wainscoting, skirting boards/baseboards, trim

These wooden surfaces can be stained or painted.
• For both surfaces, dust weekly. When dusting, be sure to spray cleaning solution on a cloth first, not directly on the surface, then dust.
• For stained wood, clean occasionally with a wood furniture cleaner. Buff dry. For nicks and scratches, use a commercial wood scratch cover. Wax all stained surfaces annually. Seal less often.
• Scratches on painted wood should be touched up with paint as necessary.

Glass surfaces

'Mirror, mirror on the wall… ' And what if all you see is a cloudy surface, smudges and water spots? Not a pretty sight. There is nothing more beautiful than clean, clear glass. It is easy to clean and you should do so at least once a month to keep it sparkling.

MIRRORS

These make an area seem larger by reflecting the height and depth of the room, and can brighten your space by bringing sunlight indoors. Position a mirror on a wall adjacent to a window for extra natural light.

Routine maintenance

• Use a commercial glass cleaner that does not contain ammonia or alcohol. Buff with a soft clean cloth or chamois leather/cloth.
• Alternatively, make a solution from 1 litre/4 cups water and ½ teaspoon vinegar or mineral spirits.
• Don't get water between the glass and the backing, this can ruin the silver surface behind the glass.
• In rooms, such as the bathroom, where mirrors can mist up, use a product designed for car windscreens/windshields containing an anti-mist agent.
• Antique mirrors should be dusted with a clean, soft, dry cloth only. Do not use any cleaners.

GLASS-TOPPED TABLES AND SHELVES

• Dust twice a week with a lint-free or chamois leather/cloth and glass cleaner.
• Avoid using abrasive cleansers or pads that will scratch the surface.
• Protect the surface of a glass-topped table with runners, trivets and coasters, when necessary.

GLASS DOORS AND WINDOWS

Cleaning frequency will depend on usage and the weather conditions. It's a good idea to have all your windows and doors professionally washed at least once a year; a good time to do this is after a season of heavy rains.

Routine maintenance

• Use any commercial glass cleaner.
• To reduce streaking, do not clean windows in the heat of the day.
• For very dirty windows, make a solution of 1 part vinegar to 1 part warm water and apply with a plastic squeegee.
• For tough stains, rub the glass with some crumpled newspaper dipped in the vinegar solution used for maintaining mirrors.

TV AND MONITOR SCREENS

• Television screens should be cleaned twice a week with a commercial glass cleaner and lint-free or chamois leather/cloth.
• Computer screens should be wiped down once a week. Check your manufacturer's recommendations for special cleaning pads for optical plastic and glass.
• Avoid using abrasive cleansers or pads that will scratch the surface.

Furniture

In our need for comfort, the furniture that we use and enjoy daily must be maintained in a manner that reflects the philosophy of our home being our castle. Dust and grime accumulate daily on all furniture surfaces, including wood, laminates, glass, chrome, leather and upholstery.

UPHOLSTERY

Regular vacuuming of upholstered furniture will help prevent soil accumulation. Do so once a week.

Spot-removal basics

• Remove excess dirt and soil promptly by scraping off any residue with a dull-edged knife or spoon, and/or blotting up spills with an absorbent cloth or thick paper towels.

• Be sure to pre-test a cleaning solution in an inconspicuous spot before using it on the upholstery.

• Do not remove the cushion from its cover when treating.

• Do not rub the spot; use a soft, white cloth or a clean sponge to apply the relevant cleaning solution.

• Rinse with a damp sponge, then dry immediately with a soft, dry cloth.

• If the spot persists, call a professional upholstery cleaner.

Spot-removal tips

Blood Because blood coagulates, it must never be in contact with anything warm or hot. To clean, mix 1 teaspoon very gentle detergent with 250 ml/ 1 cup tepid water. Alternatively, mix 1 tablespoon ammonia with 125 ml/½ cup water. Apply either solution to the spot with a clean cloth, then pat dry. Finally, sponge with clear water and pat dry.

Chewing gum, ink Sponge with a small amount of dry-cleaning solvent. Alternatively, mix 1 teaspoon very gentle detergent with 250 ml/1 cup tepid water. Apply to the spot with a clean cloth and pat dry.

Chocolate, soil Mix 1 teaspoon very gentle detergent with 250 ml/1 cup tepid water. Apply to the spot with a clean cloth and pat dry. Then, mix 1 tablespoon ammonia with 125 ml/½ cup water. Apply to the spot with a clean

cloth and pat dry. Apply the detergent and water solution again. Sponge with clear water and pat dry.

Coffee, cola drinks Mix 1 teaspoon very gentle detergent with 250 ml/1 cup tepid water. Apply to the spot with a clean cloth and pat dry. Alternatively, mix 1 part white vinegar with 2 parts tepid water. Apply to the spot with a clean cloth and pat dry. Sponge with clear water and pat dry.

Nail polish Daub with nail-polish remover (acetone) and pat dry. Alternatively, mix 1 teaspoon very gentle detergent with 250 ml/1 cup tepid water and blot with a clean cloth. Sponge with clear water and pat dry.

Soft drinks (other than cola), wine Treat as you would coffee or cola drinks (above). If necessary, go through the first step again.

WOOD FURNITURE AND CABINETRY

Your wood cabinetry can be seen as the 'furniture' on your walls, and as such should be maintained with the same amount of care and attention as your fine tables and étagères.

Routine maintenance
- Dust weekly or as necessary.
- Clean with standard furniture oil cleaner.
- Buff dry.
- For minor scratches, apply a commercial wood scratch cover.
- Wax all interior wood once a year.

Water rings
These are the white circles that are left by a wet glass that has been placed on a polished wood surface, and which can't be wiped away.
- To remove them, put 1 drop mineral spirits or rubbing alcohol on a clean cloth and massage into the water ring. Be careful not to saturate the cloth; move quickly; pat dry.
- Caution: Alcohol is not recommended for use on wood, as it can strip the surface. Use wax when you have cleaned the water ring.
- Alternatively, make a paste using 1 part bicarbonate of soda/baking soda and 1 part white, non-gel toothpaste. Put it on a clean cloth and rub gently into the water ring with a circular motion. Buff to a shine with a clean cloth.

- For stubborn stains, scrub gently with a soft nylon pad dampened with washing-up/dishwashing liquid. If the stain persists, contact a professional company for further maintenance and/or care.
- Don't risk treating the problem yourself if the furniture is valuable or French-polished. Contact your local furniture restorers' association, who will be able to help you to find a professional in your area.

PAINTED FURNITURE

- Wipe the surface with a cloth dampened in a solution made from 1 part warm water and 1 part vinegar.
- Wipe down with a water-dampened cloth.
- For stubborn stains, make a paste from bicarbonate of soda/baking soda and water. Rub gently into the water ring using a clean cloth and a circular motion. Buff to a shine with a clean cloth.
- Dust with a cloth treated with furniture polish or a duster.

LAMINATED FURNITURE

- Remove dust and debris with a cloth pre-treated with furniture polish or a duster.
- Wipe with a damp cloth using warm, soapy/sudsy water or all-purpose cleanser. Rinse thoroughly, and dry with a clean cloth.
- Do not use abrasive cleansers or pads to clean laminate, which scratches easily.

DOORKNOBS AND HARDWARE

Do not neglect the knobs and hardware on your furniture and doors, as they get a lot of wear. Time needs to be spent monthly, or more frequently as needed, in making sure they are kept well polished and clean.

Metal hardware
- Clean hinges, handles, and locks according to the metal they are made from and any special finishes they have.
- Monthly applications of wax are needed to inhibit the formation of rust. Use a standard furniture wax and apply lightly to the metal, using a soft cotton cloth.

HANDRAILS AND RAILINGS

Review all handrails once a year for necessary touch-ups. They will no doubt suffer from many knocks and scratches.

Wrought-iron handrails

• Use a soft, damp cloth for occasional dusting, but keep in mind that no regimented maintenance is necessary.

• Avoid contact with water. If wrought-iron used inside the home does come into contact with water, pat dry as soon as possible.

Wooden handrails

• Dust once a month.

• Clean with a wood preservative, as required.

• For minor nicks and scratches, apply a commercial wood scratch cover.

Lighting

The lighting in your house provides the ambiance, drama and atmosphere to each room. Maintaining the lustre of each fixture is paramount to creating the effect you most desire. Certain standard procedures apply to maintaining the light fixtures in your house. Warning: water and electricity do not mix. Be careful not to let water make contact with wires, bulbs, and sockets. A person can be severely shocked, and even electrocuted in this way.

LIGHT FIXTURES

Your home will have several different types of light fixtures, each of which requires its own cleaning procedure.

• Light bulbs should be cleaned every few months. First switch off the light, wait until it is cool and remove the bulb. Hold it at the fixing end and wipe over the glass with a barely damp cloth. Dry with a soft, lint-free cloth and replace the bulb.
• Fluorescent lighting tubes can also be cleaned, using the above method.
• To clean wall switches, first make a template from thin cardboard to go around the switch so the cleaning product does not get on the wall. Then clean according to the material. For plastic switches, use an aerosol cleaner/polish or if they are badly finger-marked, use mineral spirits on a soft cloth. For metal fixtures, use metal polish.
• Clean plastic electrical sockets with mineral spirits, after switching off the electricity at the mains. Don't get any liquid in the holes.
• Dust fixtures once a month with a long-handled tool for hard-to-reach areas.
• Removable glass, metal and plastic fixtures can be washed in warm water. Dry thoroughly before replacing.

LAMP BASES

All sorts of materials are used for lamps, from hardy metals to wood, plastic and porcelain.

• Always unplug the lamp before cleaning.
• Regular, gentle dusting with a feather or lambswool duster will take care of delicate fabrics and surfaces.
• Treated cloths are available for hardier surfaces such as brass, ceramic, porcelain, stone, wood and plastics.
• Remove and clean washable parts such as glass, ceramic, marble or plastic with a damp cloth and warm soapy/sudsy water.

LAMPSHADES

Dust your lampshades regularly with a feather duster, lambswool duster or paintbrush.

Buckram
Brush with a stiff brush if dust has become ingrained. Clean with a soft brush dipped in turpentine over the whole surface.

Glass
Dust with a feather duster and occasionally wash in washing-up/dishwashing liquid.

Parchment
Dust gently and remove marks with an India/art-gum rubber/eraser. Do not wet, or it could dissolve.

Plastic
Probably washable, so clean in soapy/sudsy water, rinse in clear water and dry thoroughly. To avoid rusting, use a sponge instead of immersing the lampshade.

Vellum
Shake together 1 part soapflakes, 1 part warm water and 2 parts methylated/mineral spirits in a screw-top jar. Wipe the lampshade with a soft cloth, then rinse with a cloth dipped in undiluted methylated/mineral spirits. Apply a thin coating of wax furniture polish and rub it in carefully.

Pleated fabric
Remove dust by dabbing with wide cellophane tape.

CHANDELIERS

These should be taken to pieces, cleaned, and re-assembled by a lighting expert.

• Rub over each piece of glass with dry chamois gloves. Try a chandelier aerosol, which you spray at the glass and leave to dry before polishing with a soft cloth.

CURTAINS AND BLINDS

Heavy dust is not attractive. Window coverings should be tackled once a year to keep them clean and dust-free. This is also important for allergy control.

Drapes, curtains and shades

Drapes are made of heavy custom fabrics, such as brocade and velvet, and are usually lined. These types of fabrics cannot be home-laundered. Curtains are usually made of cotton, linen or other washable fabric, and can either be lined or unlined.

• Vacuum weekly, using an upholstery attachment.
• Read care labels carefully; the wrong treatment can ruin or shorten the life of your window coverings.
• Launder or dry-clean curtains once a year.

Venetian blinds

• Dust with a soft, clean cloth, or vacuum using a dusting attachment once a week.
• Wash with mild all-purpose cleanser and water and a soft cloth. Rinse thoroughly, then wipe dry.
• Ammonia should never be used on aluminum.
• Unscrew and detach the blind twice a year in order to give it a thorough cleaning. The best place to do this is in the shower or by laying it out in the tub. Wearing rubber gloves, wash the blind carefully with a sponge and warm soapy/sudsy water. Rinse under the shower. Dry with a clean cloth, then air dry outside or over the shower.

Paper and bamboo blinds

• These delicate blinds should be cleaned with care. Clean weekly with a feather duster.

Duettes

Duette blinds are synthetic panels made to look like an accordion pleat. They pull up like a Roman shade.

• Dust with a soft, clean cloth or vacuum using a dusting attachment once a week.
• They can be spot-cleaned at home, but it's usually advisable to have the entire shade professionally cleaned.

Roman shades

Roman shades are sophisticated in design and easy to take care of. They come in many types of lightweight fabric and are usually lined.

• Dust regularly with an appropriate vacuum attachment.
• Blinds can be spot-cleaned at home, but always check the care label for the specific fabric.
• Roman shades can be professionally cleaned. Yearly cleaning is advisable.

Shutters

• Use a soft, damp cloth for occasional dusting, but no regimented maintenance is necessary.
• Clean wooden shutters by first removing dust and loose dirt with a long-brush vacuum attachment. Then wipe with a damp cloth.
• It is recommended that you seal all shutters once a year. If painted, repaint every few years.

Window screens

• Vacuum or gently brush with a medium-stiff brush to loosen any dirt.
• Take screens outside and hose them about three times a year, but do not use ammonia-based cleansers.

Window treatments

Your window treatments add the finishing touches to a home. There are many wonderful styles from which to choose – duettes, blinds, drapes and shutters – which will dictate, or be dictated by, the overall design of your rooms. Each of these window coverings bears a personality of its own, and has its own maintenance system.

Heating

Heating provides cosiness and warmth to your home. Ways of heating it are determined by where you live and when your house was built. A fireplace is always the most inviting, but it must be properly cleaned to maintain its appeal. Other equally effective methods of heating your home include forced air, radiators, underfloor heating and electric heaters.

FIREPLACES

Your fireplace can be the focal point of a beautifully appointed room, and as such, care needs to be taken to keep it looking lustrous and inviting to the eye.

Copper hood

• Dust and polish once every other month using a soft, non-abrasive cloth.
• In general, do not use steel wool or powdered cleansers; they can scratch the surface.
• Use a small amount of furniture wax and apply in small, circular motions.

Stone and brick surrounds

• Brush and dust as necessary.
• Scrub brick with undiluted white malt vinegar, then rinse thoroughly.
• Never use abrasive or caustic cleansing products.

Brass

• Brush off all dirt, soil particles and soot.
• Scrub clean with warm, soapy/sudsy water using a household brush.
• Rinse well with clear water.
• Dry with a clean cloth and buff.

Cast-iron

• Remove rust with a wire brush or steel wool, remembering to protect your eyes.
• Work carefully to avoid damaging any decoration.
• Use a commercial non-drip rust remover to get rid of any remaining residue.
• To prevent further rusting, apply a thin layer of vegetable oil.

Marble

• Sponge with a weak solution of mild laundry detergent. Rinse and buff dry.
• Apply marble polish if it has a polished finish.

Screens and flues

• Once a year, call a reputable chimney-cleaning service to check flues and sweep the chimney.

Wrought-iron

• Dust regularly with a clean, soft cloth.
• Lightly apply wax in small circular motions about once a month.

Metal mesh

• Dust from time to time with a medium, non-metallic brush.
• To inhibit oxidation and the formation of rust, apply a light coating of wax to the iron with a clean soft cloth. Use furniture or shoe wax, or a commercial wax for ironwork. Do not use too much wax or build-up will occur.

RADIATORS/HVAC GRILLS

Radiators/heating, ventilation, air-conditioning (HVAC) grills can look grimy from the dust blown out from the furnace or air conditioner, especially in the hard-to-reach areas behind the fixture.

Routine maintenance

• Use a vacuum cleaner attachment to clean the front and top of the fixture and as far behind as you can reach.
• Some dusting brushes are narrow enough to use behind radiators/HVAC grills; if not unwind a wire coat-hanger, make a loop at the end and tie a duster over it. Use this to get right behind the radiator.
• Wash dirty painted radiators/HVAC grills with a multi-surface cleaner. Check a small amount of the cleaner on a hidden area first to make sure it is safe to use.
• Dust grills with a soft cloth.
• If fan- or air-conditioning is used daily, dust the grills weekly; otherwise, dusting every other week is adequate.

GLEAMING KITCHENS

Your kitchen is the heart of your home – where your family's meals are prepared, stored, mixed and measured. Make it a special place, suited to your convenience, so you always know where to find what you need. Keep food fresh; pots, pans, countertops and chopping blocks meticulously cleaned and you can look forward to donning your apron and whipping up a feast with ease whenever you like.

CLEANING BASICS

• It's important to begin your day with spotlessly clean utensils and washed-down countertops.

• Glasses, dishes and sharp knives should be stored away after use to avoid breakages and nasty accidents.

• Take a look in your refrigerator to check what you will need for meals that day or week. Keep an on-going list of food and pantry items you require, so you have a complete list for the next time you do your shopping. Keep a magnetized pad on your refrigerator for this purpose, with a Velcro patch or elastic band attached to hold your pen.

• Store all kitchen cleaning products in their caddy within easy reach of appliances. An ideal place for them is under the kitchen sink, although if you have small children, ensure the cupboard has secure child-locks. It may be better to store cleaning products and other chemicals out of reach if the family is young.

• Clean up after every meal; wash countertops with a cloth dampened with warm soapy/sudsy water or disinfectant kitchen spray for tougher food spills.

• Wipe down the oven door and top of the stove-top after every use. This can be done with a cloth or paper towel dampened with a commercial window cleaner.

• Empty rubbish bins/trash cans and liners and re-line them at the end of every day. Put the excess folded plastic trash bags at the bottom of the bin before re-lining, so they will be right there for use when you need them. This same technique can also be used on the recycling bin, using large paper grocery bags for daily storage of bottles, cans and newspapers.

• When preparing meals, keep a small receptacle handy for refuse (or recycling caddy for food waste), such as trimmed fat, asparagus stalks, chicken bones and so on.

The daily routine

If time is short, the kitchen is the one room that should be kept clean over and above all the others. Food scraps, dirt and grime must be dealt with to keep the hub of the home clean and germ-free. Establish a definite routine based on your needs and those of your family, in order to keep not only an orderly kitchen, but to avoid stress and chaos around mealtimes.

Kitchen appliances

The kitchen remains the central part of the home. Appliances vary from house to house, depending on individual needs. Kitchen appliances are convenient and easy to use, and help us in our everyday tasks, but to get the best use out of them they must be cleaned regularly. Make it a habit to wipe down exterior surfaces of all appliances after each use and sanitize the interiors regularly, according to the manufacturer's instructions.

REFRIGERATOR

Your refrigerator needs to be kept rigorously clean and hygienic. Here are the basic recommendations for upkeep:

Daily

• Check all fresh food items for spoilage and throw out anything that has spoiled.
• Check expiration dates on cheese, eggs and milk; throw out what has expired.
• Wipe up liquid spills or food particles with a scrupulously clean, damp cloth – not the one used to clean the counter or the floor!
• Make sure that all leftover foods are stored in sterilized airtight glass or plastic containers.
• Wipe the door handle. For stubborn stains, use a disinfectant spray or a paste made from 2 parts bicarbonate of soda/baking soda and 1 part water.

Weekly

• Clean the inside of the refrigerator with a sponge and hot, soapy/sudsy water.
• Remove the shelves and wash them in the sink with hot water and detergent. Rinse and dry.
• Wipe the door compartments and the insides of the refrigerator with a solution made from 2 tablespoons bicarbonate of soda/baking soda and 1 litre/quart warm water. Rinse and dry.
• Wash the door seal with a mild detergent and warm water. Rinse and dry. Apply petroleum jelly occasionally.
• Remove the produce drawers and wash them in the sink with warm water and a mild detergent or a bicarbonate of soda/baking soda paste as with the door compartments.

• Wash the freezer compartment with the bicarbonate of soda/baking soda paste used for the door compartments. Rinse and dry.

Monthly

• Vacuum the condenser coils at the back of the refrigerator if they are exposed.
• Defrost the freezer. Some freezers today are self-defrosting; but you may need to defrost your freezer manually. Empty the freezer and turn it off. Put bowls of boiling water inside, and as it defrosts, wipe out the water.

DISHWASHER

Invented by a housewife, the dishwasher saves time and water as well as sanitizing dishes better than washing by hand, thanks to the use of powerful detergents and high-pressured hot water. After each use, empty debris from the trap located inside at the bottom of the machine. Use white vinegar in an empty cycle occasionally to remove mineral deposits, and refill the rinse solution regularly.

Dishwasher loading tips

Plastic containers and utensils Put on the upper rack or they will melt. Use the silverware basket for small plastic items that may fall through.
Pots and pans Put on the lower rack. Fill the dishwasher, but don't overcrowd it. Use the 'rinse and hold' setting if the dishwasher is not full. When full, select the 'pot scrubbing' cycle.
Cups and glasses Load these on the prongs to avoid breakages. Don't wedge small glasses in between other items. Don't machine-wash fragile glassware/stemware or bone china cups. These should be hand-washed in cool soapy/sudsy water.
Cookie sheets and platters Load vertically at the sides of the lower rack. Never wedge them in over other items, or none of the items will get clean.
Cutlery/flatware Mix items by type to prevent 'nesting.' Point sharp knives downward.
Plates and bowls Put on the upper or lower rack between the holders. Don't force or wedge them in over other items.

WASHING DISHES

There is something therapeutic about washing the dishes: your hands immersed in hot, soapy/sudsy water and all your dirty dishes emerging bright and sparkling. Even if you own a dishwasher there are some items; glasses with fragile stems, bone china cups and cast-iron skillets; that should be washed by hand. There is a science to washing dishes that, if followed, will keep this task as short and hygienic as possible.

Dishwashing tips

• Soak any badly soiled utensils or pots immediately in hot water, or hot, soapy/sudsy water if greasy, so they can stand while you're eating your meal. Don't soak wood or silver items.

• Scrape food off all the dirty dishes into a food waste bin or plastic bag, using a wooden or rubber spatula.

• Stack all items to be washed on one side of the sink in the order in which they are to be washed, starting with the cleanest items and working through to the greasiest ones. The order is as follows: glasses; silver or cutlery/flatware; bowls, plates, cups and saucers; serving dishes; pots, pans, skillets, casserole dishes and finally cooking utensils.

• Set up a dish-draining rack and a draining mat on the opposite side of the sink so water drains back into the sink.

• Establish a place to rinse the dishes: either the other section of the double sink, or a separate dishwashing bowl.

• Fill your sink or bowl no more than two-thirds full with water as hot as your hands can stand. If you wear rubber gloves, not only will you protect your hands, you will be able to use hotter water.

• Add liquid detergent to the water.

• Starting with the cleanest, wash similar items together to avoid any breakages.

• Don't over-fill the bowl or sink.

• Use a clean dishcloth, brush, sponge or pot-scourer to remove dirt and grease. Replace your cleaning tool as soon as it gets dirty.

• Rinse the dishes in hot running water or dip them into hot water.

• Drain the items on the dish-draining rack so that water drains off them, not into them.

• Change the water as soon as it gets too dirty, oily, too cool or lacks suds.

• Let items air dry or dry them with a clean, fresh dish towel. Some items are better if wiped with a dish towel, such as glassware/stemware and pots made from stainless-steel and aluminium, because they tend to look spotted or streaked if they are left to air dry.

• Put items away as soon as they are dry to prevent them from getting splashed or knocked.

• When you've finished, clean the bowl with liquid detergent and rinse, wash the sink and empty the drain basket, then sanitize the drain.

Helpful hint:
Keep some hand lotion within easy access of the kitchen sink so you can apply some immediately after doing the dishes.

KITCHEN DRAINS

The methods that follow will help you keep your drains clean and clear to prevent clogs, unpleasant odours and unsanitary conditions.

Avoiding clogged-up drains

• Purchase a drain strainer, which fits over the plughole. This is available from hardware stores. It allows water to drain through it, but will catch any food particles.
• Grease and oil cause clogging. Be sure never to pour leftover fat down the drain. Instead, pour it into a can or jar, cover well and refrigerate, then throw it out once solidified.
• While you are cooking, keep a very small rubbish bin/ trash can for food debris close by. Any kitchen store should have one. Line it with the smallest liner available and use it for discarding cooking scraps. After you have finished preparing your meal, remove the liner and discard it, and put in a new one.
• To prevent a build-up of grease in the sink and waste pipes, flush once a week with a solution made from 250 g/ 1 cup washing soda crystals and 625 ml/2½ cups hot water. Alternatively, use a commercial drain cleanser.

Homemade drain cleansers

These homemade cleansers are for regular drain maintenance, to prevent clogged drains.
To clean and deodorize Pour 150 g/¾ cup bicarbonate of soda/baking soda down the drain and then slowly drip warm water into it. Alternatively, mix 150 g/¾ cup washing soda in 4 litres/1 gallon warm water. First, pour hot water down the drain, then pour the solution, followed by more hot water. Use every 2 weeks.
To disinfect and sanitize Stir together just less than 250 ml/1 cup chlorine bleach, 1 tablespoon powdered laundry detergent and 4 litres/1 gallon warm water. Pour the solution into the sink, let it drain, then rinse with warm water. Do this once a month.

Homemade cleansers for clogged drains:

• Pour 125 g/½ cup bicarbonate of soda/baking soda down the drain, followed by 250 ml/1 cup vinegar. Alternatively, mix 2 teaspoons ammonia with 1 litre/quart boiling water and pour down the drain. Plunge after either solution.
• Eco-friendly enzymatic drain openers can be put down the drain. These are freeze-dried blocks of bacillus bacteria, which eat the material clogging your plumbing.

WASTE/GARBAGE DISPOSAL UNITS

Disposal units grind away food debris for safe disposal through the pipes. The following tips will keep the unit hygienic and safe to use.

Routine maintenance

• Clean after every time you dispose of food. Use a long-handled brush, hot running water and detergent, after switching off the mains.
• With fibrous food, such as artichoke leaves or asparagus stalks, toss in small amounts at a time under running water.
• Never put in large bones; but smaller bones will help to scour the grinding chamber.
• Never overload.
• Run for 10 seconds after grinding ends.
• Once you put food in, grind it immediately. Don't allow food to just sit there and rot.
• Many disposals don't accommodate cooking grease. It's better to pour it into an empty can, cover, refrigerate, then throw it out once solidified.
• If your disposal is clogged, don't throw in corrosives or drain-cleaning chemicals, or anything acid-based, such as lemon juice or vinegar. These may damage the plumbing. Enzyme products can sometimes help.

Cleaning tips

1. To rinse, put a few centimetres/1 inch of cold water in the sink. Turn on the unit and let the water run through.
2. Occasionally scour the cutting blades by filling the disposal unit with ice; turn it on; as the ice crushes, turn on the hot tap/faucet fully, until the ice melts and the water flows down. Turn off the tap/faucet, then the disposal unit.
3. Heat 6 litres/quarts water until very hot but not boiling. Add 250 ml/1 cup chlorine bleach and mix well. Pour the solution down the disposal unit. Do not rinse. Diluted bleach won't damage the plumbing but will kill fungus, mould, mildew and bacteria. After using the bleach solution, avoid using the disposal unit and drain for at least 12 hours.

STOVE-TOPS AND GRIDDLES

Stove-tops are used daily, whatever your cooking habits, and soon get grimy. A healthy practice is to wipe up spills immediately and wipe down the area daily with a damp cloth, to prevent fires or other accidents from occurring. Keep flammables away from cooktops as much as possible.

Stove-tops and gas burner grates

Made of baked-on enamel, stainless steel or black glass.

• To clean, wait until the stove is cool.
• Remove drip pans and soak in hot, soapy/sudsy water.
• Spray the surface of the stove-top with an all-purpose cleanser or a solution made from 1 part vinegar to 1 part water.
• Wipe with a sponge or clean cloth. Wipe excess away with a paper towel.
• Use a bicarbonate of soda/baking soda paste on tough spots. Wipe down with a damp sponge.
• Scour pans with a nylon-type, non-scratching pad, if necessary. Dry with a thick paper towel.

Electric hobs

Hobs are usually made of hard, heavy-duty plastic or synthetic material.

• Hobs can be taken off and immersed in a bowl of hot, soapy/sudsy water.
• For tougher-to-clean caked-on oil and scum, use an old toothbrush soaked in liquid scouring cleanser and water.

Glass-sealed hobs

• Wait until the stove-top is cool.
• Spray with a general-purpose cleanser or clean with a solution made from 1 part vinegar to 1 part water.

• Wipe with a sponge or clean cloth.
• Apply a bicarbonate of soda/baking soda paste, scrub gently and rinse.

Gas griddles

• The cast aluminum griddle has a non-stick coating for easy cleaning. For best results, the manufacturer recommends that you wash the surface with hot, soapy/sudsy water, rinse and dry.
• Do not use steel wool or coarse scouring pads or powders.
• The non-stick surface requires periodic conditioning to preserve the easy-release quality of the surface. Condition the non-stick surface with cooking oil and wipe off excess.
• When cooking, use plastic, wooden or bamboo utensils, not metal ones, which have a tendency to scratch the non-stick coating.

OVEN

Clean your oven once a week if you cook every day and every 2 weeks if you cook less frequently. Having a sparkling-clean oven keeps your kitchen sweet-smelling, and prevents your food from smelling of yesterday's leftovers.

Outside of the oven

• For stainless-steel panels, use a specialized stainless-steel cleanser. Remove finger marks with a soft cloth and a few drops of baby oil or rinse aid.
• If your oven panel is glass, you can spray with window cleaner or a multisurface kitchen cleaner.
• Soak grates, knobs and drip pans in hot, soapy/sudsy water. Use a stiff brush to remove any burnt-on soil.

Self-cleaning ovens

• Refer to your manual for details of the self-cleaning mechanism.
• Most standard ovens need about 4 hours to be thoroughly cleaned.
• A quick wipe with a clean, dry cloth afterwards is all that is needed.

Cleaning ovens manually

• Your oven should be cleaned according to the type of linings or cleaning systems it has. Refer to your manual for specific directions.
• Always wear rubber gloves and make sure the kitchen is well-ventilated.
• To remove baked-on food remnants, first pry off whatever you can with the side of a dull-edged knife.
• For normal oven maintenance, use hot, soapy/sudsy water.
• For easy-to-clean areas, use regular detergent or liquid cleanser.
• Spray stubborn remaining spots with a commercial or homemade oven cleaner and use a scouring pad.
• If you don't have time to clean the oven during the day, you can leave the oven to clean overnight. First, make sure the oven is turned off and inaccessible to children or pets. Loosen grime with a dull-edged knife. Fill a small bowl with ammonia and place inside the oven overnight. In the morning, open the kitchen windows for ventilation, then wipe out the oven with thick paper towels.

Easy oven-cleaning process

This process is for use on untreated enamel linings only. Do not use on self-cleaning or non-stick ovens.

• Wet the inside surfaces of the oven and sprinkle with bicarbonate of soda/baking soda.

- Rub with steel wool pad.
- Wipe off grime with a soft cloth.
- Repeat if necessary.
- Rinse well and dry.
- Save the commercial oven cleaner for the burned-on mess. It is more caustic.

STAINLESS-STEEL HOODS

Clean your cooker/range hood every day if you cook once a day, and every few days if you cook less frequently. In the process of taking away smoke and fumes from the kitchen, hoods accumulate deposits that need to be cleaned on a regular basis in order to keep the area immaculately clean.

Routine maintenance
- Use a stainless-steel cleanser or solution made from 4 tablespoons bicarbonate of soda/baking soda in 250 ml/1 cup warm water to clean the outside of the hood.
- Mix a little ammonia into a solution of warm, soapy/sudsy water or simply use warm water. Dip a soft cloth in either solution and use to wipe the inside of the hood. Rinse off.
- Use the ammonia solution on cool light bulbs, then rinse and dry.
- Use the ammonia solution on blades. Rinse, then air dry before putting back inside the hood.
- Having a yearly cleaning crew to take apart the fan is a good idea, but you can do this yourself as long as you are careful when dismantling it.

Sinks and taps/faucets

Your kitchen sink and taps/faucets should gleam all day long. It's not hard to keep them looking this way. After each use, wipe them down; it will only take a few seconds of your time. Water spots mar the aesthetics of your kitchen and stains can set into your sink, which can make it harder and more time-consuming to clean later on.

STAINLESS-STEEL SINKS

Many sink manufacturers sell their own cleaning products and you should follow their instructions for care and maintenance.

Routine maintenance
• Clean daily with a solution made from 4 tablespoons bicarbonate of soda/baking soda dissolved in 1 litre/quart water. Wipe dry with a clean cloth and polish with a dry cloth.
• Alternatively, use a water-based, non-abrasive stainless-steel cleanser; rinse and dry.
• Do not use abrasive cleansers or bleach, which can pit the surface.
• Wipe up any acidic spills, like lemon and tomato juice, immediately. These can discolour the finish of the sink.
• Remove streaks and water spots with a cloth dampened with isopropyl alcohol; then let air dry.
• If you live in a hard water area, use a limescale/mineral deposit cleaner once a week.
• Check that the specific cleanser is safe to use in food preparation areas.

Treating scratches
• If scratches occur, use a commercial stain-remover.
• Buff the damaged areas with a soft cloth. Buff in a lateral motion, back and forth, making sure you move in the direction of the grain of the stainless-steel.

ENAMEL AND CERAMIC SINKS

Enamel is usually cast-iron or mild steel with a glass-like finish. Ceramic sinks, also known as 'fireclay sinks', are hard, non-porous and easy to care for.

Routine maintenance
• Clean daily with a non-abrasive cleanser. Alternatively, clean with a solution made from 4 tablespoons bicarbonate of soda/baking soda and 1 litre/4 cups water. Dry with a clean cloth and polish with a dry cloth.
• Do not use bleach or abrasives.

Treating scratches
• Scratches cannot be taken out. However, these sinks can be reglazed. Contact a local enamel resurfacing company.

COMPOSITE SINKS

These are made from a combination of an acrylic substance with added mineral particles, such as silica, quartz or granite, which add strength and colour. Corian® is one brand.

Routine maintenance
• Clean daily with a solution made from 4 tablespoons bicarbonate of soda/baking soda and 1 litre/4 cups water. Wipe dry with a clean cloth and polish with a dry cloth.
• Alternatively, use a damp cloth and some washing-up/dishwashing liquid.
• For stubborn stains, use an application of white vinegar or lemon juice or a cream cleanser.

TAPS/FAUCETS

Wipe taps/faucets after each use to prevent water spots or stains.

Polished chrome
• Clean with mild soap and water and a soft sponge; dry with a soft, clean cloth.
• Do not use abrasives. To clean stubborn spots, use a non-abrasive liquid or paste polish.
• Remove rust or hard-water deposits with a mixture of 1 part white vinegar or lemon juice and 1 part water, or a commercial cleanser.

CERAMIC TILES

Available either glazed or unglazed, they look stylish and are easy to clean. Choose tiles that are a suitable grade for a countertop, they should be vitrified and sealed with an epoxy grout. Basic maintenance with water and a mild cleanser will prolong the life of the tiles. A gentle rub with a towel will restore some shine. Avoid damaging grout with acids or oils, and remember to clean spills promptly.

Routine maintenance
• Wipe down after each use with a damp cloth and some washing-up/dishwashing liquid.
• Wash weekly with a slightly abrasive cream cleaner. Rinse with clear water and a clean cloth.
• Spray with an antibacterial kitchen spray if food is being placed on the countertop.
• Polish dull surfaces with a towel.
• If grouting becomes dirty, clean with a solution of 1 part bleach to 4 parts water. Use an old toothbrush to get between the tiles. Wipe with a damp cloth and let air-dry.
• Prompt clean-up of spills prevents stains and soils from hardening and becoming difficult to remove at a later date.

Stain removal
• First, scrape off as much of the stain as possible using a putty knife or other tool that will not scratch the countertop.
• Apply a ready-made poultice to the stain (available at stone dealers or online).
• For difficult organic stains, use a solution of 1 part water to 1 part bleach. Brush the solution on the stain and leave it until the stain disappears. Hose down with water toward the drain.

GRANITE

Its durability, as well as its many colour variations, makes granite a natural choice for countertops. Less expensive and easier to maintain than marble, granite offers the luxury of stone on a daily basis. However, the surface is prone to scratching and chipping, so you need to treat it with care.

Routine maintenance
• Clean as needed with a few drops of liquid detergent and water, using only a soft sponge. Alternatively, use an all-purpose cleanser with an antibacterial agent. Do not rinse.
• Granite is difficult to stain and undiluted washing-up/dishwashing liquid should be enough to get rid of most spots. Contact a professional stone cleaner for serious stain removal and polishing.
• Every 2–3 years, apply a penetrating sealant/sealer, available at stone dealers and DIY stores.
• Avoid abrasive cleansers, which can scratch the surface. Avoid ammonia and non-chlorine bleach, which can dull the appearance of granite.

CORIAN®

Corian® is a synthetic material commonly used for kitchen countertops. It is ideal for this purpose because it is very easy to clean and maintain. It is beautiful, seamless and comes in a variety of colours. Extreme care must be taken when using a knife for cutting – use a wood cutting-block to protect the countertop.

Routine maintenance
• Wipe down after each use with a sponge and warm, soapy/sudsy water or an all-purpose cleanser with an antibacterial agent. Do not rinse.
• Remove stubborn stains with a damp sponge and a slightly abrasive cream cleanser or bleach.
• Occasionally wipe matte-finish sinks with a solution of 1 teaspoon non-chlorine bleach and 1 litre/quart hot water.

Stain removal
• To remove stains, rub matte finishes with a dampened green nylon pad and some bicarbonate of soda/baking soda or a cream cleanser. For satin finishes, use a semi-abrasive sponge pad.
• For hard-to-remove stains, gently rub a piece of medium-grade/200–300-grit sandpaper over the area, followed by fine-grade/800-grit sandpaper. Buff well to restore shine. In cases of severe damage, contact the manufacturer.

Countertops
and splashbacks

These can be made of many different materials and styles. Choosing the best countertop for your home depends on your personal preferences and projected usage. The information here will help you choose and maintain the beauty of your countertop.You may prefer the easy maintenance of Corian® or granite, or a butcher-block functionality – or maybe the more traditional look of ceramic tiles.

STAINLESS-STEEL

One of the most commonly used hard metals, stainless-steel offers durability, a smooth surface and a professional look. Stainless-steel can scratch, but is easy to maintain with regular cleaning. There are many excellent stainless-steel conditioners on the market that will keep your countertop glowing.

Routine maintenance

• Wipe down after each use with a sponge and warm, soapy/sudsy water or an all-purpose cleanser with an antibacterial agent. Do not rinse. Be sure to check that the cleanser is safe for use on food preparation surfaces.
• Remove finger marks with a soft cloth and a few drops of baby oil or cooking oil.

Treating scratches

• Use a commercial stainless-steel cleanser to treat any scratches.
• To regrain any damaged areas, buff in a lateral motion, back and forth, with a soft cloth. Be sure to move in the direction of the grain of the metal.

LAMINATE

Formica is the most popular brand, but there are newer, more expensive laminates on the market that are more durable. Do not cut anything on laminate or you will scratch the surface. If light scratches appear, use a special laminate repairer and sealant/sealer.

Routine maintenance

• Wipe down after each use with a clean cloth dampened with warm, soapy/sudsy water, or use an all-purpose cleanser with an antibacterial agent. Do not rinse.
• Remove stains with undiluted multisurface liquid cleanser or cream cleanser, using a damp cloth. Use a slightly abrasive cream cleanser or diluted bleach solution on stubborn stains.

WOOD

Wood is a renewable resource that comes in a variety of natural colours, patterns and hardnesses. Frequently used throughout the house, wood contributes a softness and warmth to the home. Clean and dust regularly. Seal surfaces that will be exposed to water.

Routine maintenance

• Wipe down with a damp cloth every few days.
• Clean frequently with a commercial wood cleaner and buff dry.
• For minor nicks and scratches, apply a wood scratch cover to the surface.

WOOD BUTCHER BLOCKS

These require careful cleaning and sanitation to prevent bacteria from becoming trapped in the crevices and causing food poisoning or serious illness. Sanitize by rubbing with the cut side of half a lemon or use an antibacterial spray.

Routine maintenance

• Clean the surface thoroughly after each use to minimize bacterial growth. Scrub the board with hot water and detergent after each use. Pay particular attention to any deep scratches where bacteria can accumulate.
• The surface can be rubbed with mineral oil periodically when the wood appears to be drying out, but treat it at least once a year, regardless of the amount of use. You can find it at most fine hardware or DIY stores.
• It is worth investing in waxed, quilted squares or plastic boards that absorb all meat juices. These can be sterilized or tossed out after use.

Cabinets

An immaculate kitchen will have spotless panels on its cabinets and drawers. In addition to food preparation surfaces, these often-forgotten areas also need to be kept clean to prevent bacterial growth.

WOOD PANELS

These are easy to keep clean. If the panels are near enough to the stove-top to get splashed by oil or other cooking materials, you will need to clean them more thoroughly, more frequently.

Routine maintenance
- Dust once a week with a damp cloth.
- Clean with a commercial wood cleaner and buff dry.
- For minor nicks and scratches, apply a wood scratch cover to the surface.
- Do not use scouring pads or powdered cleansers because they can damage the finish of the wood.

METAL AND GLASS PANELS

These require very little maintenance to free them of dust and streaks. Any other debris should be removed immediately to prevent pitting, scratching or discolouration. Their appearance will make all the difference to the feel of the room.

Routine maintenance
- Clean once a week, or when smudged.
- Use any standard glass cleaner, all-purpose cleanser or a soapy/sudsy water solution.
- Avoid using cleansers with abrasive agents.

LAMINATE PANELS

Laminate is one of the most forgiving materials, which is why it's such a popular choice for kitchens.

Routine maintenance
- Dust when needed with a dry, clean cloth.
- For smudges, apply window cleaner with a clean cloth. Alternatively, use a diluted vinegar solution.
- Do not treat with harsh cleansers.

Floors

Keeping your kitchen floor immaculate will enhance the appearance of the room and help prevent accidents from happening. From immediate wiping up of spills to regular cleaning, the following tips will help you to keep your kitchen floor as safe and clean as possible.

FIRED CLAY TILES

Unglazed tiled floors don't show wear and tear like wood and marble, which makes them highly suitable for the kitchen. There are many types of tiled floors and they are easy to maintain.

Routine maintenance
• Sweep up dirt and soil particles every day with an angled broom, antistatic mop or vacuum.
• Clean with a mild detergent and water using a soft mop.

GRANITE AND STONE

Gently clean stone on a weekly basis. Wipe up spills immediately, as most stone stains easily. Poultices can be used on stains, but prevention is better than repair.

Routine maintenance
• Sweep loose dirt, food remnants and debris every day with an angled broom, antistatic mop or vacuum.
• Clean with mild detergent and water using a soft mop.
• To remove grease and oil, use a commercial stain remover.
• Vacuum well once a week.

VINYL

Mopping vinyl regularly with a clean cloth and mild detergent will take care of most dirt and dust. If you want extra protection against germs, add a few drops of disinfectant to the water. Remember to keep sharp objects away from the surface of the vinyl because they will scratch.

Routine maintenance
• Sweep up dirt and soil particles every day with an angled broom, antistatic mop or vacuum.
• Mix 125 ml/½ cup ammonia per 4 litres/1 gallon water and mop the floor with this solution.
• Do not use harsh cleansers, mop-and-shine products or paste wax, which leave a film residue.
• Vacuum well once a week.
• To remove scuff marks, use a cloth dipped in undiluted liquid detergent or turpentine and rinse well.

LINOLEUM

A resilient floor covering, linoleum stands up well to the wear and tear suffered by a kitchen floor, making it a perfect choice for this room.

Routine maintenance
• Sweep loose dirt, food remnants and debris every day with an angled broom, antistatic mop, or vacuum.
• Wash with soapy/sudsy water and a sponge mop. Rinse with clear water and buff dry.
• You can wax with paste or liquid wax.

HARDWOOD

These floors need constant care to prevent scratches and maintain their beauty. This is particularly true when used in the kitchen, where spilled water, if left untended, can warp the wood. Seal or use a commercial wood floor cleaner once a week after vacuuming. It's also a good idea to keep a non-slip/non-skid mat on the floor in front of the sink to catch water spills.

Routine maintenance
• Sweep up dirt and soil particles with an angled broom, antistatic mop or vacuum.
• Damp-mop with an almost-dry mop.
• Once a week, vacuum well.
• Clean with a commercial wood-floor cleaner.
• On sealed floors, use warm, soapy/sudsy water.
• Do not use wax on floors coated with polyurethane or urethane.
• Do not use furniture sprays or oils; they will make floors slippery.

Helpful hint:
To prevent odours, always rinse pots and pans after use with a solution made from water, detergent and bicarbonate of soda/ baking soda.

ALUMINIUM POTS AND PANS

Light, a good conductor of heat and easy to clean, aluminium makes a great choice of material for pots and pans. Avoid bleach, acidic foods or foods containing milk or eggs coming into contact with aluminium, because these can damage the metal.

Routine maintenance
• Wash in warm, soapy/sudsy water, but make sure your detergent contains no ammonia.
• If you can't get the stains out, wash aluminium pots and pans in a solution made from 1 litre/quart boiling water and 50 ml/2 oz. white vinegar. Alternatively, nearly fill the pot or pan with water and add 2 tablespoons cream of tartar or 125 ml/½ cup white vinegar per 1 litre/quart water. Bring the solution to a boil and simmer for 10 minutes. Wash the pot in hot, soapy/sudsy water, then dry it.

Harmful substances
• All acidic substances, such as silver dips, chlorine bleach, ammonia, undiluted dishwasher detergent (powder or liquid), denture cleaners and salty liquids can damage aluminium items; avoid them.
• Overheating will streak the surface. Remove streaks with a stainless-steel cleaner.

STAINLESS-STEEL POTS AND PANS

Stainless-steel is the most commonly used type of kitchenware. It distributes the heat evenly and is easy to maintain.

Routine maintenance
• Wash in hot, soapy/sudsy water.
• Wipe the pans with a soft cloth dipped in white vinegar.
• To remove mineral deposits, fill the pot with water, add 125 ml/½ cup white vinegar. Bring to a boil, then simmer for 1 hour.
• To remove any exterior rainbow heat marks, use a commercial stainless-steel cleaner.
• To remove burnt-on deposits, boil a solution of 1 tablespoon biological washing detergent per 1 litre/quart water in the pot for 10 minutes. Repeat if necessary; wash thoroughly.

NON-STICK POTS AND PANS

Non-stick materials are extremely fragile. Their coated top layer can easily scratch, but it is also easy to clean.

Routine maintenance
• Use only plastic, wood or bamboo utensils.
• Wash in warm, soapy/sudsy water.
• Avoid abrasive cleansers or hard scouring pads.

Pots, pans and utensils

From the most basic kitchen to the fully equipped dream kitchen, pots and pans are an essential feature, as are certain utensils. You don't need every gadget that comes along, but you do need a few basic items. By maintaining your pots, pans, and utensils properly, you will not only prevent odours and damage, you will also extend the life of your equipment.

CHROME POTS AND PANS

Chrome is a plate finish for brass metal. Simple maintenance includes dusting and occasional washing with a gentle cleaner. Do not use metal polishes, spray polishes or acidic cleaners.

Routine maintenance
• Wash in warm, soapy/sudsy water.

CAST-IRON SKILLETS AND GRIDDLES

Cast-iron is an alloy of moulded iron, carbon and silicone. It is a tough and rigid substance which will darken with use. Cast-iron needs to be seasoned before use to prevent rust. First wash in warm water. Brush the surface with oil and heat in the oven at 150°C (300°F) Gas 2 for 1 hour.

Routine maintenance
• Never soak cast-iron, as it can rust.
• Dry cast-iron items thoroughly to prevent rust.
• Sprinkle the surface with sea salt, and rub with a paper towel to break up stubborn grease spots without damaging the pan's seasoned patina.
• For cast-iron items in the kitchen, other than pots and pans, treat like wrought-iron.
• Use a drop of household oil on hinges, locks and hardware.
• Use stove polish as a rust preventative for cast-iron stove parts.

PORCELAIN AND ENAMELLED CAST-IRON

French stew pots and roasting ovens are made from enamelled cast-iron. They are known for their durability and capacity to conduct heat, and come in many colours.

Routine maintenance
• Treat carefully with gentle cleansers and soft cleansing pads.
• Clean in warm water with washing-up/dishwashing liquid.
• Use a nylon brush that will not scratch.
• For persistent food remnants or spots, scrub with a sponge and undiluted liquid detergent.
• To treat stains, mix 1 tablespoon bleach in 1 litre/quart warm water and let stand, covered, for 1 hour. Then wash thoroughly with hot water and detergent, and rinse well.

Burned or baked-on material
• Use a dull-edged knife to remove as much food matter as possible.
• Fill the pot with soapy/sudsy water and leave overnight.
• For stubborn matter, spray with all-purpose cleanser and leave overnight.

COPPER, BRASS AND BRONZE

Copper is a harder metal than silver, though still soft. Brass is an even harder alloy of copper and zinc, with a golden colour. Bronze is the hardest alloy of copper and tin, which has a reddish-gold hue.

Treating corrosion

• Wash in a warm solution of liquid detergent, brush gently with a soft brush, rinse and dry with a soft cloth. Then apply a commercial cream or liquid cleanser.
• For heavier tarnishing, use a copper or brass buffer impregnated with polish. Don't use it too often; it is abrasive.
• Alternatively, rub the surface with half a lemon dipped in salt. Rinse with clear water and buff dry with a soft cloth. This will bring out the orange colour.

PEWTER

Pewter is rust-resistant. It reacts to acid, so avoid acidic cleaners. Old pewter can contain lead, which will contaminate food.

Routine maintenance

• Do not wash in a dishwasher. Hand-wash in hot, soapy/sudsy water. Alternatively, mix 2 tablespoons ammonia with 1 litre/quart soapy/sudsy water.
• Rinse with hot water, then dry gently with a cloth to buff.
• Use a cotton bud/swab for indentations, curlicues or curves.
• Never use harsh polish.
• If it is heavily tarnished, use a commercial silver cleaner.

SILVER

Silver is a semi-soft metal. Maintaining its appearance requires regular cleaning, gentle polishing and protective covers. The cleaning methods and suggestions that follow will help you keep your silverware free from tarnish for years to come.

Routine maintenance

• Remove dust with a soft cloth slightly moistened with water.
• Wash silver before polishing. Hand-wash in warm, soapy/sudsy water. Rinse and rub dry immediately to prevent spotting. Do not rub too hard or you will scratch the surface. Use straight, even strokes.
• Make sure silver is never left wet. It will turn black.
• Do not wash in a dishwasher.
• Use a polish specifically for silver. 'All-metal' cleaners contain abrasives or solvents for other metal types, which can damage silver.
• Dips or electrolytic cleaners remove the surface layer or plating.
• Store silver in flannel cloths, bags or drawer liners conditioned with silver nitrate or other chemicals. Polish just before use.
• Store infrequently used items in cupboards rather than on open shelves or racks in order to keep them clean.
• Rinse off any extraneous polish.
• Shine silver with a clean, soft cloth.

BEAUTIFUL BATHROOMS

The measure of a well-kept home can be found in its bathrooms. They should be spotless, germ-free, shiny and sweet-smelling. Keeping your family healthy begins by maintaining a well-supplied bathroom, devoid of mildew, soap scum and mineral stains. This is also your sacred space – a place to which you can retreat to relax. Make it your haven with specially chosen scents, towels and draperies.

The daily routine

It doesn't take much time to keep your bathroom spotless and glowing. For general maintenance, just a few minutes every day will usually suffice. Wipe the shower and sink(s) after each use, if you have time. Keep cleaning products tucked away in their caddy inside a cabinet for a quick sanitizing of the toilet.

CLEANING BASICS

• Frequency of cleaning should not vary.

• Use separate cleaning cloths, tools or sponges for those areas with high populations of germs and bacteria – the toilet, toilet lid and floor or cabinet walls near the toilet. As a general rule, move from low contamination areas to high ones.

• Frequently-used toilets should be cleaned every day. Use a clean cloth and a spray disinfectant to wipe down the rim of the bowl and seat. Use a brush and a standard toilet bowl liquid or gel cleanser for the toilet bowl. Gels are better because they stay in contact with the bowl for longer.

• Bathtubs that are used frequently should be wiped down daily.

• Invest in a 'catch-all' for your shower drain – a plastic strainer that goes over the drain to catch hair as you shower. This will prevent the drain from getting blocked.

• Keep a plastic squeegee in the shower to wipe off the glass and tiles immediately after showering to prevent nasty water spots from appearing. If the squeegee is on hand, you won't need to search for it.

• Keep a clean, soft cloth or sponge available to wipe off the sinks and the countertops.

• Store a dry cloth in a caddy in a cabinet to polish any chrome fixtures after use. This will prevent water spotting, which is more difficult to remove if left to air dry.

• Keep a mirror cleaner and a disinfectant spray handy.

• In order to maintain good air quality, it is essential to ventilate your bathroom as soon as it has been used. Opening the windows after you shower is the best form of ventilation. It's also a good idea to invest in a good fan system in the toilet area. Air fresheners are effective, too, but nothing beats fresh air.

TOILETS AND BIDETS

Okay, so it's not the nicest job in the world, but it needs to be done, and can be done simply. There are many good toilet cleaners to choose from; always keep one stored close by for a quick sanitizing of the toilet. This should be done daily – and is a simple task if you have a toilet-bowl brush and caddy stored right next to the toilet.

Routine maintenance
• Clean outside the toilet bowl with a disinfectant cleanser.

• Toilet-bowl cleansers of all sorts will not harm vitreous china toilets.
• Use rubber gloves to protect your hands while cleaning.
• Sprinkle a powdered cleanser into the toilet and scrub with a stiff nylon brush.
• For stubborn spots, use navel jelly or undiluted liquid detergent and a soft nylon-bristle brush.
• In hard-water areas, use a combined cleaner and limescale/mineral deposit remover where deposits form.
• Never leave any products on for too long; otherwise, the chemicals could

penetrate the surface through worn areas or cracks in the glaze, resulting in discolouration.
• To prevent clogs, pour 250 g/1 cup bicarbonate of soda/baking soda into the toilet bowl once a week, then flush the toilet.

Disinfecting the toilet bowl
• Toilet-bowl cleaners should be used daily or at least once a week.
• Use a long-handled rim brush to clean the rim holes and to clean as far into the trap as possible to prevent limescale/mineral deposits from forming. Alternatively, use a mousse that expands under the rim.
• The use of a toilet block under the rim will keep the toilet smelling fresh and protect against germs.
• Add disinfectant to the toilet bowl and leave for 30 minutes.
• Clean the toilet brush by swirling around the toilet bowl, then let it stand in a fresh mixture of disinfectant in the toilet bowl for 20 minutes.
• While the brush is soaking, wash the toilet brush stand with disinfectant cleanser.
• Rinse the brush and replace it in its disinfected stand.

Limescale/mineral deposit removal
• Daily use of a standard toilet-bowl cleanser with built-in limescale/ mineral deposit protection should be enough to keep deposits at bay. If not, use a commercial remover for sanitaryware or a bleach solution and scrub with a long-handled brush.
• Make sure that the holes in the rim are clear for proper bowl flushing.
• Homemade mineral deposit remover: Soak a cloth in white vinegar and leave it on the trouble spot for 1 hour.

Fixtures and fittings

Your bathroom fixtures – tub, sink, bidet, shower and commode – need to be kept meticulously clean, more so than anything else in your home. A bathroom caddy holding all the necessary cleaning products and tools will make this task easier for you. A freshly scrubbed bathroom is not only inviting, it can become your haven after a hard day's work.

BIDETS

Clean the outside of the bowl with a disinfectant cleanser on a regular basis. Clean the bowl of the bidet with a bathroom disinfecting cleanser once a week, depending on usage.

Sprinkle a powdered cleanser in the bowl and scrub with a nylon brush.

Use a long-handled brush to clean the rim holes to prevent limescale/mineral deposits from forming.

In hard-water areas, use a commercial limescale/mineral deposits remover for sanitaryware where deposits may form.

TUBS AND SINKS

There are many styles and types of tubs and sinks from which to choose, such as porcelain, enamel, fibreglass and acrylic. Nothing looks more inviting than a freshly scrubbed sink or tub. Generally, a quick wipe after use will suffice to remove scum, but there are also wonderful spray-on cleaners available.

Porcelain enamel tubs and sinks
- Wash with a gentle, all-purpose cleanser.
- Remove hard-water stains with a solution of 1 part white vinegar and 1 part water, or commercial deposit remover for sanitaryware. Rinse thoroughly and dry with a cloth.

Fibreglass and acrylic tubs
- Follow the manufacturer's instructions. If they are not readily available, call any good plumbing supply store for advice on how best to clean.
- For a stubborn stain, use a nylon-bristle brush and undiluted washing-up/dishwashing liquid. Do not use abrasive cleansers.

Stainless-steel sinks
- Make a cleaning solution made from 4 tablespoons bicarbonate of soda/baking soda dissolved in 1 litre/quart water. Wipe around the sink, using a cloth dipped in this solution. Wipe dry with a clean cloth and polish with another dry cloth.
- Alternatively, clean with a powdered all-purpose cleanser and a soft sponge, as necessary, depending on usage.
- Make sure when cleaning to rub lightly with the grain.
- For tough streaks and water spots, remove with a cloth dampened with isopropyl alcohol, then let air dry.
- Do not use bleach on stainless-steel.

TAPS/FAUCETS AND SHOWER SETS

As the 'jewels' of your bathroom, your fixtures should shine. Wipe taps/faucets and shower sets after each use to prevent water spots or stains. Taps/faucets usually come in chrome, which is a plate finish for brass metal. Simple maintenance includes wiping off with a dry cloth after use, and occasional washing with a gentle cleanser. Do not use metal, spray or acidic cleansers.

Polished chrome
- Clean with mild soap and water and a soft sponge; dry with a soft, clean cloth.
- Do not use abrasives. To clean stubborn spots, use undiluted liquid detergent or a non-abrasive commercial bathroom cleanser.
- Cleaning frequency depends on usage. Weekly applications give best results.
- After polishing, apply a paste wax to add another temporary protective coat.
- To keep shower fixtures beautiful, keep them clean and dry. After you've wiped the wet tiles, use a clean, dry rag to polish the fittings. This should be done after each use in order to prevent water spots.
- Remove rust or hard-water deposits with any mildly acidic solution, such as a mixture of 1 part white vinegar or lemon juice and 1 part water, or a commercial limescale/mineral deposit remover.

SHOWER ENCLOSURES

In addition to being a relaxing, serene place in which to unwind, this small but essential space traps moisture, steam and unwanted soap build-up. To prevent scum, wipe showers after each use and clean thoroughly every week. Keep a plastic squeegee handy.

Routine maintenance
• Wipe off and rinse the shower stall and bathtub after every use.
• Wipe off dirt, grime and soap scum as necessary with water and a soft cloth. Do not use any chemicals or abrasive cleansers. If water spots don't disappear using water and a soft cloth, try a small amount of a commercial bathroom cleanser or shower spray.
• The counters and walls in shower stalls and those near bathtubs and sinks need to be cleaned thoroughly with an an all-purpose cleanser once a week to prevent a build-up of scum.
• Spray tiles and shower curtain (if plastic) with a bathroom cleanser. Wipe off, then rinse. Pat dry.
• To remove mildew from shower curtains, scrub with a bleach solution and rinse thoroughly.

Showerhead maintenance
If your showerhead is made of plastic and there is mineral build-up on it, remove the head and soak it in a mixture of 1 part vinegar and 1 part water for a few hours. Don't soak polished nickel in a vinegar–water mixture or it will tarnish. Use a commercial descaler instead but check instructions first.

PIPES AND DRAINS

Easy to forget, your pipes and drains in the sink and shower collect hair and soap scum, which can cause clogging. There are many ways in which to keep drains clear. A good prevention in the shower is to invest in a 'catch-all' strainer specially made to catch unwanted hair.

Routine maintenance
• Pour 150 g/4–8 oz. bicarbonate of soda/baking soda down the drain, followed by 125 ml/½ cup white vinegar. Cover tightly for a few minutes, then run cold water down the drain.
• Strong chemical drain cleaners are not recommended because they harm the pipes.

Clearing blocked drains
• Pull out possible blocking matter, if you can.
• Pour 125 g/½ cup bicarbonate of soda/baking soda down the drain, followed by 250 ml/1 cup vinegar. Alternatively, add a few teaspoons of ammonia to some boiling water and pour it down the drain.
• Use a plunger after either solution.
• If this doesn't work, put an enzyme drain cleaner in the drain and leave overnight.
• Repeat plunger action.
• If this doesn't work, call a plumber.

Clearing blocked toilets
• If the toilet is stopped up and overflowing, turn off the water. Do not flush.
• Remove all visible waste. You may be able to clear it with a bent wire pushed around the bend. Wait until the water level drops, then flush the

toilet from a height with a bucket of water.
• If this doesn't work, take a plunger and push it sharply on to the bottom of the pan to cover the outlet. Then pump the handle up and down several times to create suction.
• If this works, flush a couple of times with the plunger in the toilet bowl to rinse it off. Wash the plunger well in soapy/sudsy water mixed with some chlorine bleach.
• If the plunger doesn't clear the pan, use a 'closet augur' or a 'plumber's snake' (available from plumbing stores) pushing the hook end in first, and working it back and forth. If this doesn't work, you may need to call a plumber or drain specialist to clear the underground drain.

MARBLE

These are highly suitable for bathrooms and look beautiful. But marble requires special care. Every little scratch or nick will show, so it should only be used in areas that get little traffic, such as your master bathroom rather than the family room. It absorbs stains and will etch from acid spills or alcohol-based products such as make-up or cleaning products. Mop up any spills at once. Keep in mind, water should be wiped up immediately, because it will leave a mark, too. Regular maintenance should include yearly deep-cleaning and buffing by a professional stone- or marble-polisher.

Routine maintenance
• Use only non-ammoniated, non-abrasive, non-acidic cleansers. Use a neutral pH soap or mineral oil.
• Apply a sealant/sealer to countertops once a year. These are available at stone dealers, DIY stores or online.

Treatment for stain removal
Water spots, rings, scratches and nicks Buff with fine, dry steel wool.
Oily make-up and bath-oil stains Mix acetone and powdered whiting into a thick paste. Daub this thickly over the stains. Tape clingfilm/plastic wrap over the poultice and leave overnight. Remove the poultice; clean off any spots. Repeat, if necessary.
Rust stains If the stain is new, rub with a clean cloth. Otherwise, mix liquid rust-remover with powdered whiting. Spread on the stain; then leave for at least 2 hours. Carefully

remove the poultice; clean off any spots with a damp rag. If this has an effect on the stain but doesn't work completely, blend the same poultice, but add some bleach to the mixture.

CORIAN®

Corian® is a synthetic surface, which is easy to maintain and is especially suited for use in a bathroom; it is beautiful, seamless, comes in many colours, and is easy to clean.

Routine maintenance
• After each use, simply wipe with a soft sponge and a liquid detergent.

Treating surface damage
• Scrub a stubborn stain with a damp sponge and some scouring powder.
• Rub matte finishes with a dampened nylon scrubbing pad and bicarbonate of soda/baking soda. For satin finishes, use a standard scouring pad.
• For minor burns and scratches, lightly sand with medium-grade/200–300-grit sandpaper. Smooth the surface with fine-grade/800-grit sandpaper, then polish with a car-wax.

LAMINATE

Formica is the most popular brand, but there are also newer, more expensive laminates on the market that are more durable.

Routine maintenance
• Wipe after each use with a sponge and a liquid-detergent solution, or spray with an all-purpose cleanser. Rinse with a clean, damp cloth.
• Do not use a dripping-wet cloth near seams in laminate surfaces.
• Do not use abrasive cleansers, steel wool or stiff brushes, which can scratch the surface.

Treating surface damage
• Apply an undiluted all-purpose cleanser to the spot with a clean cloth. Let stand; blot with a damp cloth.

PAINTED WALLS

Painted walls can easily smudge, but a drop of ammonia on a clean white cloth will remove the offending spot with a light rub.

Enamel paint
• After showering or bathing, wipe residue moisture with a dry cloth. For smudges, use a small amount of window cleaner on a dry cloth.
• Wipe down with a diluted, mild all-purpose or household cleanser.

Latex paint
• Gently wipe down walls with a clean, damp sponge, using warm water and an all-purpose cleanser. Rinse with clear water.
• For stubborn stains, use a bicarbonate of soda/baking soda paste or a small amount of ammonia on a clean cloth. Don't scrub too hard.

Walls and countertops

No matter what material you choose – tile, latex paint or one of the many kinds of stone – walls in the bathroom get scummy and damp. Periodically wipe them with a soft, clean cloth to prevent water streaks and mould. Your countertops will usually be made of polished material and can easily be maintained by wiping with a soft, dry cloth after each use.

STONE WALLS, SHOWER ENCLOSURES AND COUNTERTOPS

Stone in a bathroom is the height of elegance and beauty, and is easy to maintain. Establishing a regular routine is important in keeping the lustre of the finish. There are many types and styles of stone, such as sealed, polished and honed. Use soft sponges and gentle products to maintain the polished look.

Routine maintenance

• Clean countertops, shower floors, walls and seats with a neutral pH soap and water, using only a soft sponge. Alternatively, use a few drops of mild liquid detergent and warm water.
• The sooner water is wiped up after baths, showers and splashes, the fewer chances there will be of mineral and soap-scum build-up.
• Never use abrasive or caustic cleaning products or any solutions containing alcohol, such as ammonia, powdered cleansers, steel wool or coloured scrub pads, on stone surfaces because they will scratch and dull the surface. Avoid strong alkaline cleansers, which will eat away at the stone and turn it yellow.
• Use only non-ammoniated, non-abrasive, non-acidic cleansers.
• Perfume and make-up will damage stone surfaces. Try to keep such products well contained so that if a spillage does occur, it will be kept to a minimum.
• Rub with mineral oil every few weeks during the first year to help the stone oxidize (darken) evenly.

Treating surface damage

• Remove small scratches with fine-grade/800-grit sandpaper.

Treatment for stain removal

• You can use a ready-made poultice to remove stains (available at stone dealers) or you can make your own. To do so, first scrape off as much of the stain as possible. Make a solution from 1 part water and 1 part bleach. Brush the solution on the stain and leave it until the stain disappears. Hose down with clear water toward the drain.
• For serious stain removal and repolishing, contact a professional stone dealer.

TILED WALLS, SHOWER ENCLOSURES AND COUNTERTOPS

Creative, beautiful and easy to clean, ceramic tiling adds elegance to a bathroom. Basic maintenance with water and a mild cleanser will prolong the life of the tiles. A gentle rub with a towel will restore the shine. Clean spills promptly.

Routine maintenance

• Wipe, sponge or squeegee shower enclosures after use, then dry with a clean towel to prevent mould forming. Spray with a commercial shower spray after each use and do not rinse it off.
• Clean weekly with a detergent solution. Avoid abrasive cleansers.
• For unglazed tiles, add a few drops of liquid detergent to warm water to make a soapy solution and wash with a sponge. Rinse with water and a clean cloth.

• For glazed tiles, mix 1 cap isopropyl alcohol with 4 litres/1 gallon water. Wipe the tiles with this solution.
• For glass tiles, use a glass tile spray cleaner. Use only non-ammoniated, non-abrasive, non-acidic cleansers.
• Treat grout frequently enough to avoid soap-scum build-up; clean as needed, at least every 2 months.
• Clean dirty grouting with a soft brush dipped in a mild solution of bleach, then rinse well. Commercial grout cleaners are available from DIY stores and online. Do not use abrasive cleansers.
• Avoid oil soaps, ammonia or vinegar, which will damage the grout.
• Apply grout sealant/sealer twice a year to prevent stains.

Spot-removal guide

• Test tile and grout before applying any acidic mixtures, bleaches or scouring cleansers.
• Use a scraper or putty knife to remove debris.
• Use a nylon scrubbing pad dampened with a few drops of liquid detergent to remove stains.
• Decorative glazes or coloured grout should be cleaned with a mild, non-abrasive cleanser.
• For difficult, serious scum, coat the surface with undiluted liquid detergent, using a soft cloth saturated in the product. Wipe carefully over the tiles, leaving a thin residue. Let dry for at least 8 hours. Wet the surface with a liquid detergent and warm water solution. While the surface is wet, sprinkle on some scouring powder, then scrub with a stiff brush. Rinse with clear water and polish with a kitchen cloth.
• Occasionally, scrub grout with a brush; an old toothbrush can be used on hard-to-reach places.

CERAMIC TILES

Floors covered in ceramic tile are beautiful and easy to maintain, although they attract dust and so require frequent cleaning. Use etched tiles on the bathroom floor to prevent slipping.

Routine maintenance
• For glazed tiles, mix 1 cap isopropyl alcohol in 4 litres/1 gallon water. Wipe the floor with this solution using a mop.
• For unglazed tiles, make a soapy/sudsy solution using a few drops of liquid detergent and hot water. Mop with this, then rinse with clear water.
• Avoid oil soaps or ammonia, which will yellow grout. Avoid vinegar, which can damage grout.
• Apply grout sealant/sealer twice a year to prevent stains.

Spot-removal guide
See Tiled walls, shower enclosures and countertops, page 91.

MARBLE

Luxurious and beautiful, marble floors need to be well looked after.

Routine maintenance
• Sweep or vacuum up dirt and soil particles regularly.
• Wipe up spills with a clean, soft cloth.
• Mop at least once a week with a few drops of liquid detergent and warm water. Rinse with clear water and dry with a clean cloth.
• Apply a sealant/sealer to floors every 2 years to prevent deep stains. These are available at stone dealers, DIY stores and online.
• Do not use abrasive cleansers, which can scratch, or caustic cleaning products.
• Do not use vinegar- or lemon-based cleansers, which can etch the surface.

Treatment for stain removal
See Marble, page 88.

LIMESTONE

This is highly suitable for bathroom floors. As with most stone floors, limestone can stain and scratch easily, so it is essential to apply a good sealant/sealer to keep it looking good.

Routine maintenance
• Sweep or vacuum up dirt and soil particles regularly.
• Mop up any spills at once.
• For regular cleaning, dry-mop daily.
• Clean as needed, or at least once a week with a few drops of liquid detergent and warm water.
• Rinse with clear water and dry with a soft, clean cloth.
• Apply a sealant/sealer to floors every 2 years to prevent deep stains. These are available at stone dealers and DIY stores.
• Don't use abrasive cleansers, which can scratch, or vinegar- or lemon-based cleansers, which can etch the surface. Avoid caustic cleaning products.
• Polishing should take place every 2½–3 years by a professional service.

VINYL

Vinyl is a hardy flooring product that is ideal for use in bathrooms.

Routine maintenance
• Sweep or vacuum up dirt and soil particles regularly.
• Mop at least once a week with a neutral pH soap and warm water. Alternatively, make a cleansing solution from 125 ml/½ cup ammonia and 4 litres/1 gallon water.
• Do not use detergents or abrasive cleansers.

Stain removal
• For tough stains, rub scuff marks with a nylon pad, sponge or soft nylon brush dampened with isopropyl alcohol or undiluted liquid detergent.

LINOLEUM

It is a resilient floor that will take a lot of wear. Linoleum is easy to clean, making it perfect for a family bathroom.

Routine maintenance
• Sweep with a dust mop or broom.
• Clean with soapy/sudsy water and a sponge mop.
• Rinse with clear water and buff dry with a clean cloth.
• Wax with paste or liquid wax.

OTHER FLOOR SURFACES

For other floor surfaces, *see* Floors, page 34.

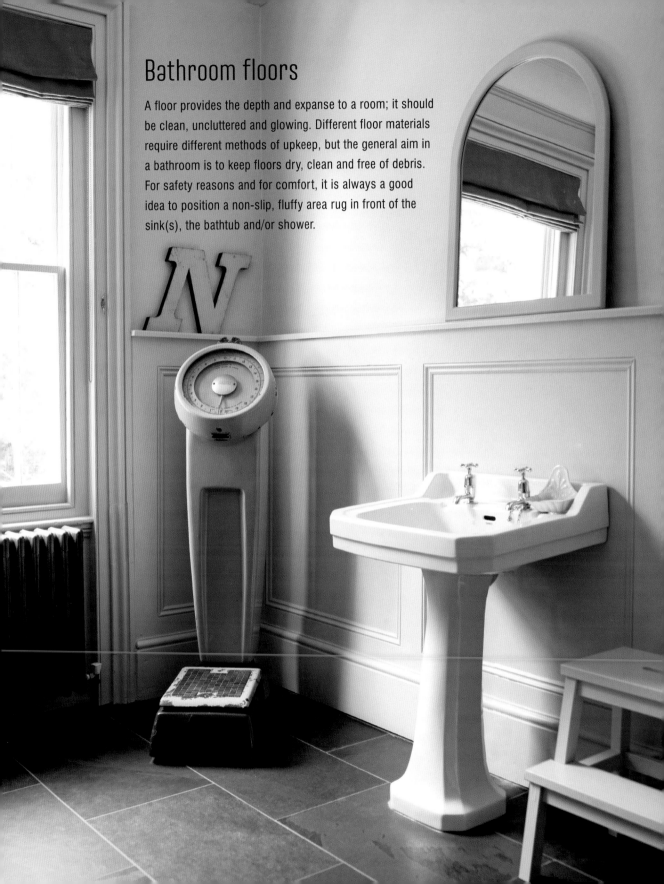

Bathroom floors

A floor provides the depth and expanse to a room; it should be clean, uncluttered and glowing. Different floor materials require different methods of upkeep, but the general aim in a bathroom is to keep floors dry, clean and free of debris. For safety reasons and for comfort, it is always a good idea to position a non-slip, fluffy area rug in front of the sink(s), the bathtub and/or shower.

LAUNDRY FRESH

Newly laundered sheets smelling of the countryside, crisply-pressed work clothes ready for the morning, and your baby's blanket fluffy and soft. They are all part of your laundry routine, and the results make you both proud and satisfied. The scent, the feel, the invitation of clean, ironed clothes, bedsheets and towels, go along way toward making a weekly chore into a pleasurable task.

Streamline your laundry

Bed linen, towels, clothes – your household's laundry can appear to be a never-ending chore. The best way to deal with it, and to maintain your sanity in the process, is to do the majority of the washing on a designated day during the week. That way, you won't be burdened with wet shirts or towels every single day.

LAUNDRY BASICS

• Schedule a major laundry day once a week. If you have a busy work schedule or want to keep your weekends free, you may need to do a few loads during the week.

• Put a laundry basket/hamper, or three-way sorter in each bedroom or bathroom.

• If you have the space it's a good idea to have separate laundry baskets/hampers for whites and lights, coloureds and darks and delicates or hand-washables.

• Separate out items that need to be dry-cleaned and put them in a closet bag.

• It's always best to treat a stain as soon as possible. However, if you are unable to get to the stain immediately, indicate its location with a safety pin before putting the item in the laundry basket, so you can find it again easily.

• If your clothes need repairing in any way, do so before washing as laundering may enlarge the tears.

• Do a full load of towels only. This will use less water, less energy and restrict lint.

• If you are using a tumble dryer, dry loads one after the other to utilize the remaining heat from the previous load.

• Always fold clothes before transporting them.

• Leave lone socks in a bag in the laundry/utility room to match with its mate later.

• Keep a few wooden, padded and rubber-clip hangers handy in the laundry/utility room or near the tumble dryer, so you can hang easily-creased items immediately after drying. This will help to prevent wrinkles from forming.

• Return wire hangers to the dry-cleaners or throw them out. Don't use them to hang up your clothes because they can ruin the shape of garments.

WASHING MACHINES

There are two types of washing machine: front-loading and top-loading. Front-loading machines consume less energy and less water than their top-loading counterparts. The most popular type of machines are front-loading automatics, which can wash around 5 kg/11 lbs., but there is a growing trend for larger capacity machines that can wash up to 8 kg/17½ lbs. In Europe, all laundry appliances are required by law to carry an EU energy label which gives details of energy and water consumption, efficiency and noise level. For optimum performance, read the manufacturer's instructions to make sure you use the right programme for each load and follow the instructions here.

Washing machine basics

• Select the appropriate programme on your machine to correspond to the type of fabric you are washing. Make sure you have selected the right programme, temperature and spin speed if the controls are separate. Don't forget to check the options available such as extra rinse, delicate or rapid wash.
• Load the drum (taking care not to overload), add the detergent and fabric conditioner to the dispenser or put the detergent directly into the drum using a dosing ball. Switch on the machine and it will stop once the cycle is complete.
• Don't machine wash items that should be hand-washed or dry-cleaned. Always check the wash care labels on garments before cleaning.
• Never overload your machine.
• Use the proper setting for the size of your load.

• Top-loading machines use more water when items are heavily soiled.
• For heavy or oily stains, use a liquid pre-wash treatment first.
• Use as high a temperature programme as possible to remove heavy stains, but don't exceed the temperature recommended for individual items.
• Use a lower temperature and reduced agitation programme (indicated by a solid or broken bar under the washing machine symbol on care labels) to reduce shrinking and fading and to pre-soak hard-to-remove stains, such as blood and food.
• If you live in a hard-water area, add a water softener to your wash.
• Match the detergent to the fabric and level of staining.
• Use in-wash stain removers or optical brighteners to whiten, brighten and clean. Proprietary whitening products will help remove yellowing on whites. Alternatively pre-soak them in a bleach solution. Be sure to check the care labels of your laundry before using bleach.
• Detergent boosters enhance the wash in cold water, hard water, or with extra-dirty laundry.
• Use liquid fabric softener in the final rinse, or add a dryer sheet to your tumble dryer, to reduce static cling and make your clothes softer.
• Add liquid starch to the final rinse for crispness.
• Clean the washing machine every few months to get clothes cleaner. Select the 95°C (200°F) cycle, add 250 ml/1 cup of white vinegar to the detergent dispenser and run an empty cycle.
• Check hoses once a year for cracks and bubbles. Replace as needed.
• Clean washer filters periodically and dryer filters after each load.

LAUNDRY ACCESSORIES

Rolling caddy for product organization

Folding drying rack or collapsible drying mesh to dry clothes that can't be tumble-dried

Trouser/pant stretchers to dry trousers/pants and make creases

Iron and ironing board

Laundry sorter and folding table

Canvas-covered collapsible hamper/laundry organizer

Water alarm: warns of possible water leak

Shelf with wardrobe-related maintenance items: sewing kit, shoe polish, rags, paper towels, spot remover, books

Container for pocket contents

Bulletin board for care labels, extra buttons, stain charts, and product samples

Trash can/bin for lint

GUIDE TO WASH CARE LABELS

Bathtub

The washing process by machine or hand

		max. temp	symbol
Cotton wash: normal (maximum) washing conditions can be used at the temperature marked		200°F	95°C ⋮⋮⋮
Synthetics/permanent wash: reduced (medium) washing conditions apply		160°F	70°C ⋯
Wool/delicate wash: much reduced (minimum) washing conditions to be used. Applies specifically to machine-washable wool products		140°F	60°C ⋮⋮
		120°F	50°C ⋯
Hand wash: do not machine wash		105°F	40°C
Do not wash		65°F–85°F	30°C ·

Triangle

Bleaching

- Chlorine bleach: a triangle indicates chlorine bleach may be used.
- Non-chlorine bleach: a triangle with two stripes indicates only non-chlorine bleach may be used.
- Do not use chlorine bleach: a triangle with a cross through it.

Iron

Ironing

- Hot iron: a maximum temperature of 210°C (390°F) may be used
- Warm iron: a maximum temperature of 160°C (300°F) may be used
- Cool iron: a maximum temperature of 120°C (230°F) may be used
- Do not iron
- Do not steam iron

Circle

Dry-cleaning

- Ⓐ Dry-clean using any type of solvent
- Ⓟ Dry-clean in any solvent, except trichloroethylene
- Ⓕ Dry-clean with petroleum solvent only
- ⊗ Do not dry-clean

- short cycle
- reduce moisture
- low heat
- no steam finishing

Square

Tumble/automatic drying

- Normal cycle: item may be tumble/automatic-dried (no heat). Maximum heat drying conditions apply
- Permanent press cycle: medium heat drying conditions apply
- Delicate/gentle cycle: minimum heat drying conditions apply
- Do not tumble dry

- ⊙ high heat
- ⊙ medium heat
- ⊙ low heat
- ● no hot air

line dry   drip dry   dry flat   do not wring

WASHING MACHINE CYCLES

Washing machines have a range of programmes and washing options to choose from. The following three programmes are the most common.

Cotton/regular cycle

A heavy duty programme (maximum/fast agitation) for cotton, denim and linen fabrics. The most common temperatures are 40°C (105°F) for light soiling and delicate cottons; 60°C (140°F) for heavier soils; and 95°C (200°F) for very heavy stains and for destroying germs. Some machines will automatically set the temperature while others have a separate temperature control. Use strong, all-purpose detergent in this cycle. Hot water is effective at removing stains most thoroughly, but it can shrink and fade your laundry. Select this program with caution.

Synthetic/permanent (easy-care) cycle

Suitable for man-made fabrics such as polyester, polycotton, nylon, viscose and blends. The wash cycle is gentler than cotton programmes so is suitable for more delicate items. Select a long pre-soak on this cycle so the cleaning can be achieved by means of the soaking process. The most common temperatures are 40°C (105°F) and 50°C (120°F).

Wool/delicate cycle

Gentler still, this programme is usually pre-set at 40°C (105°F), but some machines now have a 30°C (85°F) cycle. Slow, short movement and spin on the delicate cycle protects your finest materials from friction and snags. Unless the care label clearly states 'Dry-clean only,' this cycle can be used for the following fabrics: silk, wool, viscose, rayon, acrylic, modacrylic, acetate, lace, tulle, anything sheer, woven or knitted. Use lingerie detergent available from the lingerie department of a department store.

Other programmes and options

Anti-crease cycle The drum tumbles the load intermittently for up to 30 minutes after washing.

Drip dry/no spin Washes without spinning for delicate items.

Economy options Reduces the wash temperature or length of the programme.

Extra rinse Added water ensures all detergent is removed.

Freshen-up option This is a rinse with a fabric conditioner for delicate clothing.

HAND-WASHING

The most delicate fabrics need to be washed by hand instead of in a washing machine. Always read the wash care label to check how an item should be washed. It is recommended to use a specialized detergent for hand-washing, which will be gentler on delicate fabrics than standard detergents. Such products are readily available.

How to wash by hand

• Put some cool-to-tepid water in a sink or washing-up bowl and add some specialized hand-washing detergent (see the packaging for the recommended amount to use).

• Gently move the item back and forth through the water, then rinse thoroughly in cool, clear water.

• Do not wring, squeeze any excess water out gently by patting the item between two clean, colourfast towels.

• Dry the item flat or on a hanging rack. If hanging it on a rack with clips, make sure you don't clip the delicate parts of the item or you might stretch or damage it. Instead, loop the item around the clips.

NON-STANDARD WASHABLES

Certain items, because of the fabric or their size, need to be treated on an individual basis. Follow the care labels to determine how to wash them. Always test for colourfastness (see page 103).

Plastic shower curtains and draperies

Scrub with a sponge soaked in a solution made from detergent and hot water. To remove mildew, add a little bleach to the water or use an anti-mildew spray cleaner.

Leather gloves and mittens

Do not wash suede or lined leather gloves. Clean the outside with a soft, wet cloth, then with a proprietary leather and suede cleaner available from shoe retailers or online.

Lingerie, undergarments and foundations

See Hand-washing, above. To machine wash, put tights, stockings and other delicate items in a net lingerie bag. Fasten bras to prevent snagging. Select the delicate/wool programme and use a non-biological detergent. Avoid chlorine bleach. Dry flat or on a hanging rack.

WASHING DETERGENTS, SOAPS AND OTHER ADDITIVES

Buying a washing powder or detergent used to involve simply selecting a brand and size; now you have to choose between shelves of different products. The word 'free' on a detergent means that nothing has been added to it, no dyes, scents and so on. 'Heavy-duty' and 'all-purpose' products can be used on all clothes and linens, except for delicates. 'Ultra' indicates that the product is concentrated, so only use half the volume of normal detergents. Always read the instructions on the detergent packet and use as recommended, and test fabrics for colourfastness when using additives (see opposite).

Conventional powders

These are for either machine or hand-washing (don't confuse the two: if hand-washing powder is used in a machine it will produce too much foam and harm the machine). The active ingredients include surfactants which attack dirt, builders that hold the dirt in the water, phosphates, bleaches and optical whiteners. There are two types of powder: biological and non-biological. Biological powders contain enzymes which help to break down stains at lower temperatures. Non-biological powders don't contain enzymes.

Mild/speciality detergents

With a neutral or near-neutral pH, these work less well on stains than stronger detergents, but are best for use on delicate fabrics and baby clothes.

Enzyme-based laundry and pre soak/pre-wash products

Excellent for getting rid of protein-based spots, such as bodily excretions, dairy products, grass stains and chocolate. Let the garment soak in the solution for at least 1 hour before washing.

Fabric softeners

These will fluff up the material and reduce static cling and creasing to make ironing easier. Softeners can build up in the fibres and eventually become less effective. Avoid use in every wash. Don't use fabric softeners on flame-retardant garments, because they reduce the effectiveness of the special treatment.

Optical brighteners

These are found in nearly all detergents and oxygen- or all-fabric bleaches to make white or coloured material look crisper and brighter in daylight.

Whiteners/brighteners

Continued washings can fade or alter the colour of clothes. Whiteners and brighteners will prevent fading, whiten whites and restore colour. They are available separately or as additives to laundry detergents.

Bleach

Bleaching is a process by which dark or coloured pigments are made to dissolve in the wash. Chlorine bleaches whiten and disinfect material, but can strip fibres and discolour hues. They will damage silk, wool, leather, mohair, nylon, elastic, resin-treated and flame-retardant materials. Oxygen bleach pre-treatment sticks are excellent for fine material, including washable white wool and silk, and can be used on stains up to one week before the item is washed.

BLEACHING WHITE WASHABLE WOOL AND SILK

Soak the item in a solution made from 1 part hydrogen peroxide and 4 parts lukewarm water.

Soak wool for 10 minutes, silk for 30 minutes.

Rinse in your machine on a setting for delicate fabrics and washable wool and silk.

TEST FOR COLOURFASTNESS

When you are washing a garment for the first time, especially a delicate item, always test for colourfastness before washing.

Whites

• Always wash whites separately from coloured items to avoid dye transferring onto the whites.
• Do not bleach delicate items which specifically state 'no bleach'.
• Chlorine bleach can bring out crisp whiteness and remove stubborn spots on white clothes.
• If your white clothes have a coloured trim, test the trim for colour change before using bleach (see previous).

Colours

• Always separate dark colours from light ones before washing.

• Test for possible 'bleeding'. Materials to test are denim, tie-dyed clothes, handpainted items and Indian gauzes.
• Fabrics that can continue to bleed are denim, and clothes coloured with madras and natural vegetable dyes.
• Always use a detergent recommended for coloured fabrics.

Detergent

To test whether a fabric is colourfast with your detergent, do the following:
1. Add 1 teaspoon detergent to 250 ml/1 cup warm or hot water.
2. Immerse a corner of the garment in the solution.
3. Press onto a clean white cloth, strong paper towel or tissues.
4. If nothing bleeds, rinse, let dry and test again. If the fabric bleeds or the cloth is stained, dry-clean the garment.

Chlorine bleach (sodium hypochlorite)

To test whether a fabric is colourfast with chlorine bleach, do the following:
1. Add 1 tablespoon bleach to 250 ml/ 1 cup cool water.
2. Apply to a hidden underseam of the garment.
3. Wait at least 1 minute.
4. Dab with a clean white cloth.
5. Check for yellowing.
6. After rinsing, dry, then check again.

Other wash additives

To test any other washing products, make a slightly stronger solution than normal by mixing it with just a small amount of water. Test as for detergent (see previous).

Stain removal

Stains are the bane of any laundry washer's life. They can ruin clothes and household linens, but a stain doesn't have to signal the end of a garment's life. There are hundreds of stain-removing products available, it's just a matter of finding the right one.

STAIN BASICS

• First check that the garment is neither hand-wash nor dry-clean only.

• Read and follow packet instructions on all cleaning products.

• Treat stains as soon as possible as it is easier to remove new stains that haven't yet set into the fabric. If the item is dry-clean only, take it to be professionally dry-cleaned as soon as you can. Point out the stain to the dry-cleaner – mark it with a safety pin so you don't forget where it is.

• Test the stain remover on an unseen area of the item to check for colourfastness exactly as you would for a detergent (see page 103). Rinse.

• When using bleach, bleach the entire item to prevent uneven colour.

• Place the stained material face down on a clean cloth or paper towels when working to remove the stain.

• Put the stain remover on the reverse side of the stain.

• Dry-cleaning solvents should never go into your washing machine as they are flammable. Always rinse garments after applying such solvents and let them air dry before putting them in the washing machine.

• Use stain removers cautiously and separately from other detergents.

• Always wash clothes after you have treated them with stain removers.

• If there is any bleach in the stain remover, be cautious and check the wash care label on the material you are treating to see if it is safe to use. If it isn't, try all-purpose or oxygen bleach instead.

COMMON PROBLEM STAINS

The 'oops' of eating, the stains from everyday use, the little accidents that happen when we work and play and the stains that result can ruin our clothes. However, the information below should give you a fighting chance. If the directions call for bleach, but your fabric is coloured, make sure you use a colour-safe bleach or a specific stain remover.

Cosmetics

Foundation Soak using a pre-wash detergent, then machine wash at as high a temperature as the fabric will allow. For stubborn marks, treat with a stain remover or liquid detergent: work into the dampened stain until the outline of the stain is gone, then rinse. If an oily spot persists, treat with a biological detergent. Rinse and wash as normal.

Deodorants, antiperspirants Treat with a liquid detergent, then wash as normal. If more treatment is needed, use a pre-wash stain remover. Use a biological powder and in-wash stain remover.

Lipstick Soak in a detergent solution, then dab with a proprietary stain remover. Sponge with a detergent solution, then wash as normal.

Nail polish This is very difficult to remove. However you can try nail polish remover (but never use it on synthetic fabrics). Place the stained garment, stain side down, on paper towels and soak with nail polish remover. Replace the paper towels frequently as the stain will run into it. Repeat until the stain is gone. Rinse, then wash as normal.

Perfume Apply stain remover to the affected area; then launder.

Detergent stains

Spotting To prevent this, check you are using the correct dosage of detergent in your machine. Dissolve the detergent before placing items in your machine; pre-soak extra-soiled clothes and rinse thoroughly.

Blue spots These come from bluing agents or fabric softener. Remove by soaking in hot water, then running through a second wash.

Light spots These come from brighteners. Soak in a solution of 1 part detergent to 2 parts warm water for 2 hours, then machine-wash, but without adding detergent. If the light spots come from bleach, there is nothing you can do.

Brown spots or streaks These come from minerals in the water. Remove with rust remover or a solution of 1 part lemon juice or white vinegar to 1 part warm water.

Fabric softener Wet spot and treat with bar soap. Rinse, then wash. If spot persists, sponge the area with rubbing alcohol or dry-cleaning solution. Rinse well and wash.

Environmental stains

Grass First, treat with a proprietary grass stain remover. Then machine wash using a biological detergent.

Mud Let dry, then remove as much of the caked mud as possible. Wash at the hottest temperature allowed for the fabric using a biological powder and in-wash stain remover. Repeat the process if necessary.

Pollen To remove surface pollen, dab with adhesive tape or use a vacuum cleaner nozzle/tip on low suction. Treat with a proprietary grass stain remover, then wash as normal.

Pine resin Rub the spot with dry-cleaning fluid; allow to air dry. Work in detergent and wash as usual. If stain won't go away, pour on a few drops of ammonia. Let dry. Wash in liquid laundry detergent.

Foods

Baby formula Soak the stain in a pre-wash detergent for a few hours. Wash as normal.

Beverages (tea, coffee, soft drinks, sodas, white wine, alcoholic drinks) Soak the stain in cool water. Rub stain remover or liquid laundry detergent into the spot, then wash with a biological powder.

Chocolate This should come out if you machine wash using a biological powder.

Coffee and tea (black or with sugar/sweetener) Run the stain under cool water immediately, if possible, then treat the stain with detergent and wash with a biological powder.

Coffee and tea (with milk/cream only – no sugar) Sponge the stain with warm water. Apply liquid detergent, then wash in the hottest water allowed for the fabric, using a biological powder.

Dairy-based products Treat with a stain bar or soak in a pre-soak product for 30 minutes if the stain is fresh, or for several hours for older stains. After soaking, wash as normal.

Egg Make a solution from 150 g/ ¾ cup of biological powder per 4 litres/7 cups of cool water. Soak the stain in this solution for 30 minutes for a recent stain or for several hours for an older stain. Wash the garment as normal.

Fruit juices Soak the item in cool water and then treat with a proprietary fruit and wine stain remover. You might need to bleach white fabrics in order to get the best finish possible.

Tomato ketchup/sauce Rinse the item in cold water, then soak in a solution made from 150 g/¾ cup of detergent per 4 litres/7 cups of cool water for about 30 minutes. Wash as normal with a biological detergent.

Mustard First treat the spot with a pre-wash stain remover, then machine wash with a biological detergent.

Red wine Act immediately. Never cover the stain with salt as this will set the stain. A traditional solution is to pour on sparkling or soda water. Soak a clean, white cloth with water and douse the stain liberally with it. Then use a clean, dry cloth to blot dry. Treat dried stains with a stain remover or a solution of hydrogen peroxide.

Human excretions

Blood Let a recently stained garment sit in cold water for one hour. Work liquid detergent into any remaining stain. Rinse, then wash. Treat a dried spot in a warm biological detergent solution, then wash as normal. If stain remains, wash again.

Urine, vomit, mucus, or faeces Machine wash at as high a temperature as the fabric will allow using biological powder. If the odour persists after washing, use a fabric deodorizer.

Ink

Fountain pen ink Dab fresh stains with milk or hold them under cold running water until they have gone, then wash using a biological powder. Use bleach on older stains on white fabrics or a proprietary stain remover on coloured fabrics.

Ballpoint ink Put the spot face down on a white cloth to absorb most of the stain. Try holding the garment under cold running water until the pigments are gone. Rub liquid detergent into the stain, then rinse. Repeat if necessary. Soak in warm water and add 1–4 tablespoons of ammonia per 1 litre/1¾ cups of water. Rinse well. Wash at a high temperature and use bleach, if the fabric will allow it.

Felt-tip or drawing/India ink Usually indelible, drawing ink can usually not be washed out.

Laundry stains

Collar and cuff soils Treat with a stain bar or specialist spray for collars and cuffs and let sit for 30 minutes, or longer, then wash as normal.

Dye run/transfer (white material that has picked up bleeding dye from other garment) Use a commercial colour run remover. Wash as normal. If the stain persists, soak the item in bleach and wash again. For coloured fabrics and delicate whites that cannot be bleached, soak in a biological detergent solution, then wash. To minimize dye transfers, remove items from the washing machine as soon as the programme is finished.

Perspiration Apply a proprietary stain remover. Wash in the hottest water allowed for the fabric in question. Pre-treat stubborn stains with a stain remover, then wash using a biological powder.

Mildew Treat old stains on white fabric with a bleach solution or a specialist stain remover for mould

and mildew. If some soil persists, apply a hydrogen peroxide solution. Rinse and wash as normal. Let air dry in direct sunlight.

Yellowing of white cottons or linens Wash at as high a temperature as allowed for the fabric using a biological powder plus a proprietary whitening product (see page 102).

Yellowing of white nylon Let the item sit overnight in a pre-wash product or 'oxygen bleach' (see page 102). Wash in hot water with a biological powder, checking the wash care symbol for the hottest water temperature recommended for the fabric you are treating.

Paint, gum and other difficult matter

Chewing gum or adhesive tape Treat with ice to harden the matter for easy removal and rub off with the edge of a spatula. Saturate with stain remover. Rinse, then run through your washing machine as normal.

Grease (cooking oil and fats, motor oils) Light soil can be pre-treated with a spray stain remover, liquid washing detergent or a pre-wash product. Wash in the hottest water allowed for the material. Put ingrained spots face down on clean paper towels. Apply a proprietary stain remover to the back of the stain and change the paper towels regularly. Let air dry, then rinse. Wash the garment in the hottest water possible.

Paint A stain caused by water-based emulsion paint should be soaked in warm water before it sets, then wash as normal. This kind of stain most often cannot be treated when dry. For oil-based paints, including varnish, use the solvent listed on the label as thinner. If there is no label

information, use turpentine. Rinse. Pre-treat with stain remover or detergent. Rinse and wash. This is very unlikely to be removed.

Rust Use a commercial rust and iron-mould remover. Treat immediately as it can spread to other garments.

Scorch It is impossible to remove heavy scorch marks because the fabric has been denatured.

Shoe polish To remove liquid shoe polish, apply a paste of powdered detergent and water, then wash. Use the edge of a spatula to remove any remaining shoe polish and paste from the material. Pre-treat with a stain remover, then rinse. Work in detergent to moisten the spot, then wash using a biological powder.

Tar Do not let the stain set. Use the edge of a spatula to remove excess tar. Place soiled surface smudge side-down on paper towels. Pat down with dry-cleaning fluid. Change towels often. Wash in hot water.

Tobacco Wet the spot and work in bar soap, then rinse. Use a stain bar or soak in a biological detergent solution. Wash as normal. If the spot persists, soak in a hydrogen peroxide solution and wash again.

Pet stains

Hairballs Scoop up the mess with paper towels and discard. Spray the stain with a commercial pet stain remover (available from vets and pet stores) and spread into the fabric with the tips of your fingers. Wait a minute, then rub vigorously with a clean cloth.

Pet faeces and urine Remove faeces with a paper towel and discard. On carpet or upholstery, treat the stain with a commercial stain remover and rub in with fingertips. Rub with a clean white cloth until the stain is gone.

Wash your carpet and upholstery at least three times a year. If your pet makes a habit of defecating or urinating on the bed or on a favourite item of yours, machine-wash the sheets or item with non-toxic stain and odour remover.

Waxy build-up

Candle wax and crayon Treat with ice, then remove any surface wax with a spatula. Sandwich the wax stain between paper towels and use a warm iron to melt the wax. Change paper towels frequently. Sponge the remaining stain with a stain remover. Let dry, then wash.

Drying

Once you've washed your laundry, spin dry to remove as much water as possible. Line drying will give you the freshest smelling results, but a tumble dryer or drying rack is often most convenient, especially in wet weather.

TUMBLE/AUTOMATIC DRYER

Before you choose a tumble/automatic dryer, you need to consider where you will put it. A condenser model can be sited anywhere as it doesn't have a hose. A vented model has a hose that channels the steam outside via a hole in a wall or through a window.

Tumble/automatic-drying basics

• It is best to underdry rather than overdry. More sophisticated sensor dryers have moisture sensing strips or 'electronic drying' that automatically turn the machine off when the required level of dryness is reached.
• Add enough items to provide proper tumbling, but never overfill the dryer. You want proper ventilation to give even drying throughout, without wrinkling. Full-sized dryers will dry a load of about 5 kg/11 lbs.
• Clothes that require specific washing temperatures usually require similar drying temperatures. Use the highest heat setting for cotton, denim and linens, a low or delicate temperature setting for synthetics, fine knits and anything that will snag.
• Tumble dryers can wear off elastics and rubber on items such as fitted sheets. You may want to line dry such items occasionally to prolong their life.

• It is important to check the lint filter and empty it after every load as too much lint in your dryer can cause a fire. Empty the dryer hose once a year. To do this, remove the hose from the machine and thread an old towel through it.
• If you have a condenser dryer empty the water container after each use.
• Remove items from the dryer as soon as the cycle has finished. The items should still have a trace of dampness.
• Hang or fold items as soon as you take them out of the dryer to prevent wrinkles forming. Have on hand a few plastic hangers on which to place or fold the clothes.
• To condition flat-dried clothes, 'air-fluff' them on a cool air setting. This will prevent them from becoming stiff.
• If clean clothes are wrinkled, put them in the dryer with a moistened, lint-free towel on a low temperature setting for 5–10 minutes.

DRIP-DRYING

• Light cottons, polyesters, silk and items that do not stretch can be hung to dry. Otherwise, dry flat.
• Hang jackets, blouses, sweaters and dresses (unless marked 'dry flat') on hangers that fit their shape and allow them to drape properly. Make sure the shoulders of the hangers are nicely rounded.
• Make sure you close buttons or zips correctly. Smooth collars, seams, trim and pockets.
• Use collapsible drying racks or a hanging rack for lingerie, hosiery and other items that do not need hangers.

DO NOT TUMBLE/AUTOMATIC DRY:

Heat-sensitive fabrics
Polypropylene
Acetate
Acrylic
Elastane
Spandex
Plastic
Hosiery
Drip-dry materials
Rayon viscose
Some knits
Wool

DRYING FLAT

Many knits and woollens have care labels indicating that the item needs to 'dry flat'. If this is the case, make sure you do so otherwise you risk stretching or mis-shaping the fabric.

• Find a flat area away from sunlight and lay the item flat on a clean, well pressed white sheet. Make sure the area is well ventilated and away from pets and children.

• Items dried flat often need to be 'air dried' for 5 minutes in the tumble dryer to prevent stiffness. Check the wash care symbol on the garment before putting it in the tumble dryer.

LINE-DRYING

If you have a garden or backyard, this is the best way to dry your laundry. The image of clean sheets and linens drying in the wind conjures up sunny days and fresh laundry.

Bras Pin by the hooked end.
Dresses Pin by the shoulder.
Full skirts Pin by the hem.
Pillowcases Pin one side only, leaving remaining side to hang open.
Sheets Fold hem to hem over the line and pin by the corners.
Shirts Hang by the tail, and always unbuttoned.
Socks Pin by the toe.
Straight skirts and pants Pin by the waistband.
Towels Pin at the corners.
T-shirts Pin by the hem.
Underwear Fold over the line and pin.

Ironing and pressing

What more pleasing sight is there than a neatly folded pile of freshly-ironed laundry? With pristine clothes in your wardrobe/closet, clean sheets on the bed and fresh bathroom and dish towels on hand, you will feel revived and your home will look luxurious. There are certain items of clothing and household linen that need to be ironed while others do not; you can't wear a shirt or finely embroidered blouse that isn't ironed, but you can live without linens or sheets being ironed – although that can be one of life's little luxuries! Delicate fabrics should be pressed rather than ironed to prevent them getting crushed, stretched, damaged or becoming shiny. Tailored suits as well as garments made from wool, silk, rayon, netting and pile fabrics should all be pressed rather than ironed.

IRONING BASICS

- Make sure your ironing board is well padded and that the cover is clean.
- Your iron soleplate should be clean and residue/rust-free (see previous).
- Wait until the iron is hot enough to steam the water before beginning.
- Check the wash care label and always use the correct temperature setting on the iron for each particular item.
- Test the heat on a hidden area of material first, such as the underside of a hem, to avoid scorching your garments.
- Put the item on the ironing board and flatten it out.
- Use one hand to keep the garment straight while the other hand moves the iron.
- Move the iron lightly but deliberately in a sliding motion over the fabric.
- Never leave the hot plate of the iron facing downwards. Always set the iron on its stand when you let it rest.
- Iron garments needing the lowest setting first and progress to those needing the highest. Use the one-dot setting for acrylic, silk, nylon polyamide, acetate and polyester; the two-dot setting for polyester blends and wool; and the three-dot setting for cotton, linen, viscose and denim.
- Iron thicker areas of the garment first in order to avoid creasing the thinner, more delicate parts as you continue to iron the rest of the garment.
- Have on hand a spray bottle or a sponge for sprinkling or dabbing water, and spraying starches.
- Cottons and linens should be sprinkled with water one hour before ironing. Iron while still damp, using a hot-steam iron setting. Flatwork should be sprinkled on one side only. Two-sided items, such as clothing and pillowcases, should be sprinkled on both sides.
- Press cotton and linen items while they are still slightly damp on a hot steam setting.
- Use a cool-steam iron setting on untreated cottons, viscose and silks.
- For minimum ironing, use perma-pressed clothes and blended fabrics. Remove from the dryer as soon as the programme has finished, fluff out and fold or hang the items neatly.
- Always hang or fold laundry as soon as it is dry to minimize the creases and therefore reduce your ironing load.

PRESSING BASICS

- Whereas ironing involves 'sliding' the iron across the fabric, pressing comprises of a press and lift technique. Press the iron onto the fabric, then lift it off quickly; avoid 'sliding' the iron as much as possible.
- A pressing cloth should be used to act as a heat buffer between the iron and the fabric. This can be made from unbleached muslin or cheesecloth or you can use a clean, white towel.
- When pressing delicate fabrics, put a heavy towel (without a nap) under the item. Press on the wrong side of the fabric, using a steam iron setting or a damp pressing cloth with your iron set at medium heat.
- Wrinkles should be steamed out.

Ironing and pressing tips

Creases Iron on the wrong side first, using small strokes on collars, hems, and cuffs, while pressing out smoothly with the palm of your hand.

Damasks Iron both sides to produce a sheen on the top side.

Delicate fabrics To avoid creating a sheen on delicate fabrics, iron on the wrong side or use a clean towel as a pressing cloth. This applies to fabrics such as wool gabardine, polyester, linen, and all silks.

Embroidered or sequined fabrics Lay face-down on a cotton dish towel; then iron on the wrong side with a pressing cloth over the top of the fabric to protect patterns and delicacies.

Fringe Untangle while wet.

Gathers Iron from the outside into the gathers.

Lace and cutwork Use a pressing cloth or dish towel; don't put the iron directly on the lace.

Linen Sprinkle linen items with water, then stretch the damp linen into shape. Use a hot iron, but take care because linen can scorch quite easily. Iron on the wrong side to press the item into shape, but not to dry it. Stop ironing while there is still a suggestion of dampness in the fabric. Over-drying will increase the chance of scorching. Never iron on the right side. Hang immediately to finish drying naturally.

Napkins Iron flat. Do not iron any creases; press them instead.

Pile fabrics These fabrics should not be ironed.

Plackets Close zippers, snaps, and hooks, but not buttons, before ironing plackets. Work the iron carefully around any buttons, hooks, snaps, or zippers.

Pleats Lay or pin the pleats in place before ironing. Hold the material taut against the pressure of the iron. Iron in long strokes starting at the waist and working down to the hem.

Puffed sleeves Stuff puffed sleeves or pockets with tissue paper or a small towel before ironing.

Sheets Fold flat sheets in half; iron, then fold completely. There is no need to iron fitted sheets because they are pulled tightly over the corners of the mattress and any creases will disappear.

Stretchy fabrics Put a pressing cloth on top of the fabric and iron in the direction of the weave.

Tablecloths Round ones should be ironed in a circular motion, turning the fabric around as you iron. Fold square or rectangular tablecloths in half, wrong side facing out. Sprinkle with water, then iron on the wrong side until half-dry; refold with right side facing out, then iron on the right side until nearly dry. Press out any creases when both sides are finished.

Folding

A little time taken to care for clothes and linens is time well spent. Once they have been washed and ironed, it's worth folding them correctly so they fit in your cupboards easily, without getting crumpled. Careful folding prevents wrinkling in your clothes and sets the creases in the right places.

Shirts

1. Button first, middle, and last buttons or snaps.
2. Set face-down. Bring one sleeve across the back of the top horizontally. Fold it down vertically at the shoulder area.
3. Repeat with the other sleeve.
4. Fold the lower third up.
5. Fold the next third up. Turn the top face upward. Put away carefully in a drawer or closet.

Dresses

It is advisable to hang dresses in a wardrobe/closet. But if you can't, fold them at the waist, then tuck the sleeves in like a shirt (see above). Bring the edges of the skirt together carefully. If the skirt is long, fold it up, but not in the middle.

Handkerchiefs

Fold in a square after pressing.

Lingerie

Divide into three separate drawers: one for knickers/panties, which should be separated by colour and folded like underpants (see opposite); one for bras, which should be stored by colour and kept uncrushed, cup-side up; and one for previously-worn tights and stockings, which should be stored according to colour and thickness and folded into fourths. Use scented sachets to keep everything sweet-smelling. Keep handkerchiefs with these.

Trousers/pants and jeans/slacks

Use trouser hangers. Hang carefully by the hems, making sure to align inseam. If you do not have trouser hangers, use thick, wooden hangers and place over hanger, making sure to align the inseam.

Shorts

Align inseam and make sure pockets have been carefully flattened. Try to lay out evenly in drawer. If you must fold, fold in half.

Skirts

It is always better to hang up a skirt, either in a clip hanger or by its own loops. If you cannot, bring the edges of skirt together. If the skirt is long, fold up. Do not fold in the middle.

Socks

Never roll up into a ball. This stretches one sock, ruining its elastic, and takes up too much room. Instead, fold neatly together in half, one on top of the other.

Underpants

Fold on each side toward the middle, then in half.

HOUSEHOLD LINEN

Tablecloths

Store linen tablecloths wrapped in acid-free paper. Keep either in an acid-free container or on shelves papered with cotton sheeting. Be sure to re-fold frequently to prevent mould and creasing.

Napkins

Like tablecloths, keep in an acid-free container or on shelves papered with cotton sheeting. Never iron creasing, or mould may develop. Fold loosely into a square or rectangle, with monogram on lower left corner. You may also fold into a triangular shape, with monogram at the base of the triangle.

Helpful hint:
Save the tissue paper that lies inside items that have been dry-cleaned. Place between folded clothing or linens to prevent creasing.

Blankets

Fold in half, then flip over and repeat.

Duvet/comforter

To store, put the duvet/comforter in washed, unbleached muslin or cotton. Use tissue paper between the folds and store in an acid-free box or on a shelf lined with cotton sheeting. You can buy storage bags for duvets and blankets. Never use plastic bags, because they lock in moisture. To prevent mould and mildew, duvets must not be stored in a humid room, such as the bathroom. Heating units and direct sunlight can ruin your duvet/comforter.

Fitted sheet

Make sure both top corners of the sheet are puffed out. Fold the sheet in half horizontally. Fit the top corners into the bottom corners. Make the sides perfectly even by laying flat on the bed and smoothing down. Fold in half, horizontally, then again vertically. Lay neatly on shelf.

Flat sheet

Match the bottom edges to the top and fold in half, horizontally, pretty side out. Fold in half again, horizontally. Fold again, vertically. Larger sheets may need to be folded again, horizontally, to fit on the shelf. Pat down. Lay your fitted sheet over your flat sheet.

Pillowcases

Fold in half lengthwise, then in half again widthwise.

Towels

Fold in thirds lengthwise, then in half or thirds widthwise.

The linen closet

Keeping lovely linens makes any homemaker feel special. When your bed looks crisp, clean and all dressed up, the bedroom seems complete, while a bathroom stocked with plush towels in matching colours gives a warm, lived-in, luxurious texture to an otherwise utilitarian room.

BATHROOM LINENS

You don't need to spend a fortune on outfitting your bathroom, as there are year-round white sales to watch out for. Look out for sales at your favourite department or bed-and-bath store, then buy two sets of towels of the same colour and design. This way, you can refresh your hand towels and face cloths midway through the week. Also, if any items get damaged in any way, you know you have a replacement.

A set of towels should consist of the following:

Guest towel

Hand towel

Bath towel

Bath sheet

Washcloth

Bath mat

Choosing towels

When purchasing towels, always look for 100 per cent cotton. Check for thickness and softness. Do not buy synthetic blends. Always wash your towels in scented softener, and dry them with a softener sheet as well. The double-duty helps to keep them extra-soft and fluffy. Don't over-dry them.

BEDROOM LINENS

For the well-made bed, you will need a bottom sheet, a top sheet (even if you have a duvet/comforter), a pillowcase/cushion cover, and a cover. Keeping everything in good condition will mean your bed remains comfortable for as long as possible.

Sheets

• When buying sheets, check that they are made of an all-natural fabric with no synthetic fibres and that the thread count is at least 250 per square inch. Synthetic blends are harsh to the skin, and thread counts of 250 or less are rough – the higher the thread count, the silkier the feel. The finest-quality sheets are made from Egyptian cotton. A mixed-fibre sheet will not wrinkle, but it will be much harsher to the touch. Silk and satin sheets tend to slip off the mattress.

• Standard sheets can be bought in six different sizes: crib, twin, double, queen, king and California king (wider but shorter than a regular king-sized bed). Each size is available in two styles: flat and fitted. You will save yourself a world of trouble by purchasing fitted bottom sheets with elasticized corners that can be simply stretched over the mattress. A flat sheet has no elastic at the corners and needs to be tucked in (see page 118).

• For very thick mattresses, be sure to buy sheets bearing the essential label, 'deep pocket,' as recommended by most linen departments. You don't want to find you've bought the wrong sheets.

Covers

You will need a blanket, quilt, duvet/comforter on top of the bed to provide warmth. The one you choose is a matter of personal preference. If somebody in your household suffers from respiratory problems, you may want to invest in allergen impermeable cases. These are micro-porous mattress, pillow, and duvet or comforter protectors that allow perspiration through but keep dust-mites and droppings out. They are available from specialist stores for allergy control.

Pillowcases/cushion covers

These can be bought in many sizes to match the standard-sized pillows available: standard, queen, king, European, boudoir (baby) and neck roll. Always use a zip-up cover that goes under the pillowcase/cushion cover to protect your pillow/cushion and keep dust and allergens away.

Pillows/cushions

When a pillow/cushion flattens out and grows hard to sleep on, it is time to throw it out. A down pillow will lose vitality every 4–5 years. Feather, synthetic or foam pillows/cushions will need replacing every 1–2 years. Use allergen-proof under-covers on your pillows to protect against allergies and respiratory ailments. Although they are the most luxurious, feather and down pillows can often cause or aggravate allergies. If you are allergic to these products, alternatives are now available that use synthetic down made of polyester fibres. You can choose the type of pillow you prefer: soft, medium or extra-firm.

Mattresses

To keep your mattress in top condition, you must look after it. Follow these simple rules:

• Flip your mattresses regularly.
• When new, do this every few months.
• After 1 year, do once a year.
• Vacuum your mattress frequently.
• Clean your mattress pad and cover regularly.
• Air out your mattress twice a year for at least half a day. This will require two strong people, as it is arduous work. Carry the mattress outside to air on the patio or terrace, or prop against an open window.

Making the bed

Most sets of sheets come with a bottom sheet that is fitted to go around your mattress corners and these are easy to fit. Some expensive linens aren't available as fitted sheets. Here are the rules for making a 'military-style' bed, sometimes known as 'hospital corners'.

BED MAKING BASICS

1. Put the bottom sheet on the bed. Tuck in the bottom section of the sheet.
2. Next, tuck in one side, starting at the head of the bed and moving down to the foot. Make 'military' corners by pulling up the edge of the sheet about 30 cm/12 inches from the end of the bed. Lift it up to make a diagonal fold.
3. Lay the fold onto the mattress. Take the part of the sheet or blanket that is hanging and tuck it under the mattress.
4. Drop the fold and pull it smooth.
5. Tuck the hanging sheet under the mattress. Repeat on the other side.
6. Put the pillows/cushions at the head of the bed before adding the top sheet. Lay the top sheet on the bed with the right side face-down on the bed (so when you bring the hem down over the blanket, the right side will be face-up). The hemmed end of the top sheet should be at the headboard end of the bed, and the hem should be about a foot from the headboard when the sheet is eventually folded back.

7. Next, lay the blanket (if you are using one) right-side-up on the top sheet. The top edge should be 15–25 cm/6–10 inches from the head of the bed. Tuck in the blanket and top sheet at the foot of the bed and make 'military' corners as above. Fold the top part of the sheet over the blanket.
8. Put a light spread on top of the blanket, if needed, to keep the blanket clean and add weight and warmth.
9. If you are using a flat bedspread, you can tuck it in if it isn't too thick, or leave it hanging decoratively over the sides of the mattress. Duvets/comforters are usually left untucked, and can be folded down or left flat, extending to the headboard. Alternatively, a quilt may be used under a spread or coverlet, or decoratively as the final cover on the bed.

DUVET/COMFORTER BASICS

• A duvet/comforter should be no more than 8 cm/3 inches longer horizontally and vertically than the bedcover.
• For daily upkeep: fluff the duvet/comforter by taking hold of the top two corners and giving it a vigorous snap. Fluffing makes your duvet/comforter cosier by increasing the loft – the fuzzy clusters of down expand to fill more space and trap more warm air.
• When possible, hang it on the clothesline. The air and sun will evaporate any trapped moisture, giving the duvet/comforter a fresh scent.
• The easiest way to insert the duvet/comforter into its cover is as follows:
1. Turn the cover inside-out.
2. Put your arms inside the cover and hold onto the top corners.
3. Grab the top corners of the duvet/comforter through the cover.
4. Still holding firmly onto the corners of the cover and the duvet/comforter, shake vigorously so the cover falls down over the duvet/comforter the right way out.
5. Lay the duvet/comforter on the bed and fasten the cover.
6. Give it a thorough shake to fluff it up.

FOOD

Food is not just about sustenance, it is also about comfort, enjoyment, indulgence and sensuality. The touch of a peach, the scent of freshly baked bread, a tray of warm cookies from the oven – these are the true pleasures in life. As elsewhere in the home, hygiene, a 'living tidy' philosophy and a sensible routine will keep the storage, cooking and safety of food problem-free.

Understanding food

Nothing is more important than your health and that of your family. You need to understand the nature of the food you prepare. How fresh is the lettuce in your refrigerator? How long can you keep that jar of pickles? When should you defrost meat and what is the safest method for doing so? Most of us know some, but not all, of the answers to these important questions. To make sure you never run the risk of food poisoning, you need to know every aspect of food preparation and storage that may affect your health.

KITCHEN BASICS

• Keep a basic food checklist specific to what you cook and how you live. Know what you and your family eat on a daily, weekly and monthly basis so you know what to keep in the pantry and freezer for long-term use, in the refrigerator for weekly consumption and the fresh produce you need on a daily basis.

• Know the maximum storage times of all the foods you consume: whether it's fresh, canned, refrigerated or frozen (see page 136). Rotate your packets, cans, bottles and so on, frequently. Bring those with the earliest dates to the front of your cupboard or refrigerator so they get used first. Be aware of 'sell-by' and 'use-by' dates on all foods and always throw out those that have expired.

• Know what kitchen utensils you need. Everyone cooks – even if it's just a little and even the most rudimentary of kitchens needs basic utensils. Knowing what you need is important; it is the beginning of the formation of your very

own culinary expertise (see page 146).

• Know what dishes, silverware and glassware you need in order to entertain, and how to set the table. Even if you don't entertain often, it's good to know what you need and how to do things properly when you do have guests for dinner (see page 148).

• Check your oils, spices and herbs, as they will eventually become rancid. Herbs will dry out and lose their potency and flavour and should be tossed out. Oils will change colour after 1 month.

• It's practical to keep the items you use most frequently on your counter so they are easily available. Use attractive jars, bins, or ceramic pots to hold your tea, coffee, sugar, cereal and any other items you use on a regular basis.

• Put dried herbs and spices you use most often in an easily reached cupboard near the stove-top (see page 124, Helpful hint).

BASIC FOODS CHECKLIST

Each household will have its own specific list of foods, based on diet, food preferences and the composition of the family. A well-stocked kitchen will always have basic foods on hand that can be whipped up into easy meals. Here is a list of 'must-haves', which can be customized according to your own personal tastes.

Helpful hint:
Direct sunlight bleaches the colour and taste of herbs and spices even through glass containers, so store in the pantry away from direct sunlight.

Staples

Bicarbonate of soda/baking soda
Baking powder
Breakfast cereals
Chocolate: cocoa powder, cooking/
    baking, choc chips
Coffee
Couscous
Cream of tartar
Dried fruits
Dried lentils
Flour: plain/all-purpose, self-raising/
    self-rising and wholemeal
Noodles: egg or rice
Nuts: raw and roasted
Pastas of all types
Raisins and dates
Rice: brown, long grain/white, wild,
    risotto, basmati and pudding
Seeds: raw and roasted
Sugar: caster/granulated,
    icing/confectioners' and brown
Tea: caffeinated and herbal

Cans, cartons and jars

Cans of: chopped tomatoes, anchovies
    in oil, beans of all varieties
Coconut milk
Condiments: mayonnaise and dressings
Fish: tuna, salmon or sardines
Jams, jellies and preserves
Ketchup
Molasses
Pickles, olives and pimentos
Relish
Salsa
Soups and broths
Sweet and sour pickles
Tomato purée/paste (tubes instead

of cans to use small amounts
without waste)

Oils and vinegars

Olive oil and sunflower oil for cooking;
    sesame oil
Extra virgin olive oil for salads and
    dressings
Chilli/chile oil for flavouring
Vinegar: red and white wine vinegar,
    balsamic, tarragon

Herbs and spices

Cayenne pepper
Chilli powder
Cinnamon: ground and sticks
Coriander: ground and seeds
Cumin: ground and seeds
Curry powder
Ginger
Chilli/hot red pepper flakes or Aleppo
    flakes
Mixed herbs or herbes de Provence
Mustard powder
Nutmeg: whole
Oregano
Paprika: Hungarian
Rosemary
Thyme
Turmeric

Seasonings and flavourings

Bay leaves
Black peppercorns
Stock/bouillon cubes: vegetable,
    chicken, beef
Coarse sea salt
Flavour extracts: almond and vanilla

Honey
Mustard: Dijon, brown, French
  and wholegrain
Soy sauce
Teriyaki sauce
Worcestershire sauce

Fresh foods

Keep on hand a selection of fresh seasonal fruit and vegetables that will be used within 2–3 days of purchase. The sooner they are used, the more nutritious they are. Most fruits and vegetables may be kept on the counter depending on the temperature in the home, but should be refrigerated before they ripen fully.

Apples
Carrots: bagged last longer (buy baby carrots where possible; they taste better and their flavour lasts longer)
Celery: unwashed, stored in food bags

Fresh herbs, such as flat-leaf parsley
Garlic
Lemons: those with the smoothest skin give best juice
Limes
Onions: red, yellow, white
Oranges
Red chillies/chiles
Pears
Potatoes
Tomatoes

Refrigerated foods

Bacon: freeze unopened package after 1 week
Butter: preferably unsalted/sweet
Cheese: all types
Dry sausage: pepperoni, chorizo for soups and stews
Eggs
Fresh ginger
Green and red (bell) peppers and Jalapeño peppers

Milk: semi-skimmed/1% fat or skimmed/ skim milk for drinking and cooking
Orange juice or other fruit juice
Plain yogurt: no gelatin
Salad ingredients: lettuce or other leafy salad greens, tomatoes, spring onions/scallions, cucumber
Sour cream or crème fraîche for baked potatoes and baking

Frozen foods

Breadcrumbs (fresh tastes better; packet preserves longer)
Chopped parsley and chives for garnish
Fish
Frozen peas and other frozen vegetables, keep in resealable bags
Ice cream
Lemon and lime juice: freshly squeezed, freeze in ice-cube trays
Meat and poultry
Sliced bread
Stock/bouillon or broth

Buying fresh food

Almost all kinds of fresh foods are available in most markets year-round, allowing us the luxury of the freshest food possible most of the time. Always try to search your local farmers' market to see what local seasonal produce is available. This will be far superior to what is imported from other parts of the country or abroad. Fresh food requires minimal storage. There are important guidelines in selecting the best fresh produce: fruits, vegetable, meats, poultry and fish. There is no need for guesswork; just be aware of what to look for.

FRUITS AND VEGETABLES

In general, in selecting fresh fruits and vegetables, avoid all signs of bruising, spotting, wilting, dehydration or desiccation. Make sure to pay attention to smells; anything that smells particularly 'ripe' or overly sweet can signify the onset of rot.

Store fruit and vegetables in plastic bags rather than paper bags, as the latter accelerate maturation. The only exceptions to this are tomatoes and mushrooms, which shouldn't be stored in plastic, as it draws out the moisture and causes mould.

Vegetable	Choose	Avoid
Asparagus	narrow, succulent stalks, preferably baby stalks, and rich colouring	sagging, flat, thickened and yellowed stems, with stalky matter on the stems
Aubergine/ eggplant	skin should be perfect and smooth	blemished skin
Beetroot/beets	young, small and bright red	long, with rough spikes at the top
Broccoli	small green florets with thin, healthy stalks	yellowish buds, with thick, thready stalks
Cauliflower	full, round bouquets with few greens	florets with spots on them: it's a sign they are going over
Celery	firm, green stalks with crisp leaves	too light in colour, sagging
Cucumbers	small, green and firm	large, watery, thick-skinned, full of seeds
Mushrooms	caps should be tight, closed, and unbroken; gills should be light in colour; stems should be firm	soft, gooey, flaccid, bad smell
Onions	firmly wrapped with unbroken skins	sprouting, discolouration or wilting
Peppers (bell)	thick, glossy skin	dark spots, wilting
Potatoes	ones without eyes	any that are sprouting
Radishes	firm, red, with fresh, green leaves	too much white; shrivelled roots
Tomatoes	should be ripe and firm to the touch	signs of bruising or shrivelling
Turnips	unmarked, clean, smooth, with a uniform colour	signs of shrivelling, dark spots, limpness or mould
Winter squash and pumpkins	should be hefty; stem should be smooth and healthy green	signs of bruising, unevenness and spotting

CHOOSING FRESH FRUITS

Certain fruits can be bought slightly under-ripe as they will ripen at room temperature. These include apricots, avocados, bananas, cantaloupe, kiwi fruit, nectarines, peaches, pears, persimmons, pineapples and tomatoes. In general, unripened fruit is harder, greener or paler than ripened fruit. For quick ripening, put the fruit in a paper bag for 1–2 days. For natural ripening, place on the countertop out of the sun. The following fruits will not ripen at room temperature, so you should make sure they are ripe when you buy them: all berries, citrus fruits, grapes, dates, currants, figs and watermelons.

Fruit	Appearance	Time needed for fruit to ripen
Apricots	firm but not hard; not squishy	2–3 days
Avocados	spots mar the surface. Colour changes when ripe from pale green to brown-grey	3–5 days
Bananas	choose firm, unblemished fruit. Brown spots indicate over-ripening. Use in pudding or bread	depends on temperature. Keep in a cool, dark place, but don't refrigerate: this prevents ripening
Cherries	begin to look dehydrated when they are old	2–4 days
Cantaloupes	tend to develop mould, especially at the top and bottom, when they are turning	2–4 days
Grapefruit	the skin will change when it is too ripe; it will begin to look dehydrated and lumpy	will not ripen at room temperature, so buy only ripe fruit
Grapes	turn mouldy around the stems when they are going and emit a sickly-sweet odour	will not ripen at room temperature, so buy only ripe fruit
Honeydew melons	a ripe fruit is yellow-white to creamy in colour	2–4 days
Kiwi fruit	firm but not hard	1 week until soft but not mushy
Nectarines	become hard and desiccated when going; when ripe, they should be tender to the touch	2–3 days
Peaches	firm but not hard; should yield to light pressure	1–3 days
Pears	turn mouldy near the stem when over-ripe	2 days
Persimmons	firm but not hard; should yield to light pressure	1 week
Pineapples	give off a disagreeable, metallic scent when turning	1 week – watch for colour to change and outside to soften

MEAT AND POULTRY

Today, purchasing fresh meat and poultry is vastly different from years ago. Most of it has passed strict inspections and has been handled by trained personnel. However, you still need to look for any signs of spoilage: uneven discolouration, odour and freezer burn. Careful handling at home will reduce any chances of food poisoning.

• Keep meat in the original package until you use it. Do not rewrap, as undue handling will introduce bacteria into the product.
• Place meat in the coldest part of the refrigerator.
• Do not purchase meat that is in any way discoloured. If it discolours while in your freezer, check for ice crystals inside the package. When in doubt, it's better to discard it.
• Defrost or marinate meat in the refrigerator – never on the counter, as this breeds bacteria.
• Never thaw, then refreeze raw meat or poultry. This will cause spoilage and could even lead to food poisoning.

FISH AND SHELLFISH

When purchasing fish and especially shellfish, you must make sure that it is as fresh as possible. Always buy from a reputable fish merchant or supermarket. If shellfish is alive when you buy it and fish is fresh, you will help to avoid any possibility of food poisoning.

• Choose the freshest, firmest, most 'alive-looking' fish from your neighbourhood market or fish store. The eyes will be shiny, the scales polished. If there is anything filmy or malodorous about the fish, don't buy it; it's been around too long.
• Shellfish should still be alive when you buy it.
• Fresh fish and shellfish should be stored in their original packaging. Find the best fish merchant in your area, who receives frequent deliveries at least once a week.

> **Helpful hint:**
> Keep an opened box of bicarbonate of soda/ baking soda at the back of the refrigerator to avoid odours caused by fresh fish, cheese and other smelly products.

The storecupboard

Your larder is your own personal customized grocery store. A well-stocked larder is every cook's dream. It makes whipping up a quick meal simple and practical. Keep an eye on supplies and keep a note of anything that is running low, so you remember to buy it on your next shopping trip. A magnetized writing pad attached to the refrigerator is ideal for this.

STORAGE GUIDELINES

• Date foods and rotate them so you use the oldest ones first.
• Keep shelves clean and neat.
• Store items in transparent, airtight, moisture-proof, plastic or glass containers so you can see what's inside.
• Check packages for damage to seals or wrap and rewrap, if necessary.
• Dispose of damaged cans.
• Throw out any packages or cans with an expired date.
• Canned milk products should be inverted to prevent an accumulation at the bottom of the can.

Storage tips

Crackers If they have softened, put on a foil-lined baking sheet and heat in the oven at 220°C (425°F) Gas 7 for 4 minutes to crisp them up.
Stale bread Use in stuffing, as breadcrumbs and in bread puddings. Alternatively, cut slices of stale bread into cubes and fry in olive oil to make croutons for a salad or soup.
Brown sugar If it becomes hard, put in a microwaveable container and microwave on high power for 2 minutes.
Nuts If they have become a little stale, you can roast them. Put them on a foil-lined baking sheet and roast in the oven at 180°C (350°F) Gas 4 for 3 minutes, no more.
Potatoes Put some kitchen paper in your bag of potatoes to absorb any moisture and keep your potatoes fresh.
Strawberries Empty fresh strawberries out of their original container and put in an airtight plastic container. Put some folded kitchen paper on top of the strawberries to absorb the moisture and retard mould growth.

What can be stored in the larder?

Some of these foods will need to be refrigerated after opening (see page 133). Always check the labels on the packaging:

Baking powder and bicarbonate of soda/ baking soda	Dried pasta and noodles
Cereals	Dry mixes for cakes, desserts and soups
Chocolate, choc chips, cocoa powder	Flavour extracts
Cooking oil and salad oil	Flour (with preservatives)
Cornflour/cornstarch	Honey and syrups
Potato chips	Nuts
Dried beans, lentils, and other pulses	Raisins and dates
Dried herbs and spices	Rice
	Sugar
	Tea and coffee
	Canned and bottled foods

Containers

• Airtight and leak-proof containers are recommended. Plastic is better than cardboard.
• Store foods in their original packaging until opened unless the packaging is damaged, in which case you should rewrap the product.
• Rewrap opened food in new clingfilm/plastic wrap.
• Do not store anything in opened cans; metal leaches into food, which can be poisonous.
• Store fruits and vegetables separately in unsealed plastic bags to maintain moisture and air circulation. Sealed bags or dampness from washing accelerates mould and rotting.
• All grain products, including flour, should be stored in an airtight container to prevent staleness and possible infestation.
• Bread should be stored in a bread bin or wrapped in airtight plastic and stored at room temperature for no more than 4 days. Freeze any bread that won't be consumed within this time.

The refrigerator

Refrigerators improve our lives by allowing us to store food for longer periods of time. They have changed our choices: the way we cook, the way we eat and the way we live. But pay attention to guidelines that let you know how long you can store your food for optimum freshness.

STORAGE GUIDE

• Maintain the temperature at 0–5°C (40°F) or below.
• The door is warmest and the bottom shelf coldest (this can vary depending on the cooling system in the refrigerator – check the manufacturer's instructions or use a refrigerator thermometer).
• Store household aids, such as jarred and bottled products, in the door: batteries, nail polish, medicine, face and eye masks, condiments, delicate olive oils and gourmet salad dressings. It is advisable to keep cosmetics there as well, to give them a longer life.
• Poultry, fish and raw meat should be kept in the coldest part of your refrigerator: the bottom drawer (sometimes marked 'meats').
• Use drawers as indicated: one is usually for meat, the other one for vegetables. Use the latter to store vegetables you want to use soon, as refrigerating will crisp them up.
• The top shelf is recommended for dairy: eggs, butter, sour cream, cheese. And for tubes of refrigerator biscuit and cookie dough.
• Stock the items in an orderly fashion, with newer items behind older ones. If the older items are at the front, they will get used first.
• Don't overstock; otherwise, cool air can't circulate.
• Leave meat, poultry and fish in original wrap until use.
• Dairy products, grapes and celery take on the odours around them. Store them in airtight containers or plastic bags.
• Wash fruits and vegetables at the time of use, not before, to reduce spoilage. Fruits need less humidity than vegetables, and onions, garlic and all squash/gourd vegetables need the least humidity. Check your produce carefully every day for signs of spoilage.
• Store each type of item separately. Combining them may age them prematurely or cause a flavour change.
• Combining apples and carrots gives carrots a bitter taste. Store carrots in the vegetable bin of your refrigerator, sealed in a plastic bag. Apples can be left on the counter for a few days, then refrigerated.
• Combining apples and potatoes speeds the aging of potatoes. Store most potatoes in a dark, cool pantry. Tiny, new fingerling potatoes tend to age more quickly than the baking potato; refrigerate these.
• Tomatoes and aubergines/eggplants shorten the life of leafy greens near them.
• Refrigerate pressurized cans such as whipped cream.

FOODS REQUIRING REFRIGERATION

Some foods need to be refrigerated as a matter of course, others only after having been opened.

At all times

All dairy products
Bacon
Butter (there is often a special tray in the door)
Cheese
Coffee for optimal flavour
Dry yeast
Eggs and egg-based foods: for example, custard, dessert pots, mousse cakes
Fish
Fresh meat and meat products, such as sausages
Juice
Leftovers
Luncheon meats
Most fruits and vegetables, except bananas, grapefruit, potatoes, sweet potatoes, unripened tomatoes, onions and beans/legumes
Natural flours without preservatives
Poultry
Tofu products

After opening

All cooking oils (best refrigerated after opening, or store in cool, dark cabinet)
Baby food and formula
Canned food (store in airtight plastic containers)
Canned milk products (store in airtight plastic containers)
Coconut: canned or shredded
Grated cheese in cans
Icing/frosting
Jams and jellies
Ketchup
Maple syrup
Mayonnaise
Mustard
Nuts and seeds
Paprika, chilli/hot red pepper flakes, chilli powder
Peanut butter
Relishes and condiments
Salad dressings
Worcestershire, soy and barbecue sauce

STORAGE GUIDE

- Freeze foods not being used within guidelines for refrigeration.
- Don't overstock to allow air to circulate.
- Wrap foods in freezer wrap, label with date and contents.
- Keep the freezer temperature at -18°C (0°F) or below; the quality of frozen food deteriorates more rapidly above -18°C (0°F).
- Break large items into smaller units so you can use them as needed without having to thaw the whole package, except for meat which should be stored in its original packaging to reduce the opportunity for contamination by bacteria.
- Wrap fresh herbs in freezer wrap and store in the freezer for the long term or in the refrigerator for the short term.
- Ginger root can be frozen for up to 3 months if it is wrapped tightly in clingfilm/plastic wrap.
- Season your meat when you are preparing to cook it, not before you freeze it.
- Make sure that ice crystals do not gather inside packages of frozen foods or leftovers. To do this, double-wrap fish, chicken, and meat in butcher paper or clingfilm/plastic wrap, and put in sealed plastic bags. Put leftovers in sealed plastic bags or other freezerproof containers.
- Freezing inactivates, but does not destroy, bacteria and moulds. Once the food is thawed, the bacteria can become active and multiply quickly to levels that can lead to food-bourne illness.

Thawing foods

- When thawing frozen foods or leftovers, never leave on the countertop or in the sink: this will promote bacterial growth.
- Thawing in the refrigerator is safe but slow, requiring a full day (24 hours) for every 2.5 kg/5 lbs.
- You can cover the frozen food, unopened in a bowl of ice water. This takes 1 hour for every 1 kg/2 lbs., but you will need to change the water every half an hour. This is time-consuming and somewhat messy, and should only be done in an emergency.
- The quickest and easiest process for thawing is the microwave. The guidelines vary with each model and manufacturer. Always use the lowest power setting you can; it is better to thaw it more slowly than risk parts of the food starting to cook. Sometimes, the outer edges of thawed meat may end up rubbery. Rotate food as it thaws, and cover food with waxed paper for even distribution of heat. Always use tempered glass or ceramic containers in the microwave – never plastic (unless it claims to be microwave-safe) – it can melt. Using tempered glass is the safest choice, since many people ignore microwaving guidelines and overheat their food or do not heat it properly.

Storing leftovers

- Cool as quickly as possible – cover and let cool at room temperature.
- When cool, store all leftovers in the refrigerator in airtight, leak-proof containers, or wrap tightly in clingfilm/plastic wrap.
- Repack canned food leftovers in clean, airtight plastic or glass containers. Never store food in opened cans.
- Divide large quantities of food into smaller containers to cool faster.
- Do not refrigerate roasted meat in the same container as its stuffing, since it will spoil more quickly.

FOODS THAT SHOULDN'T BE FROZEN

All raw vegetables

All uncooked dairy products including soft cheeses, cream sauces and any baking product made with a base of eggs or milk

Some fruits can be frozen, but degrade a little and lose some flavour

The freezer

Longer-lasting storage than the pantry or refrigerator is available in our freezers, allowing us to buy and store more fresh seasonal meats, such as spring lamb and seafood. Always remember to mark each item and date it to make sure you use it within the freezing guidelines.

The food keeper

Excerpted with permission from *The Food Keeper: A Consumer Guide to Food Quality and Safe Handling*

(Developed by the Food Marketing Institute, Washington, D.C., with the Cornell University Institute of Food Science)

FOODS PURCHASED REFRIGERATED

Product	Refrigerated	Frozen
Beverages, fruit		
Juice in cartons, fruit drinks, punch	3 weeks, unopened; 7–10 days opened	8–12 months
Dairy products		
Butter	1–3 months	6–9 months
Buttermilk	1–2 weeks	3 months
Cheese, hard (Cheddar, Swiss, block Parmesan, etc.)	6 months unopened; 3–4 weeks opened	6 months
Parmesan, Cheddar, mozzarella, etc., shredded	1 month	3–4 months
Cheese, processed slices	1–2 months	Doesn't freeze well
Cheese, soft (brie, bel paese, etc.)	1 week	6 months
Cottage cheese, ricotta	1 week	Doesn't freeze well
Cream cheese	2 weeks	Doesn't freeze well
Cream, whipping, ultra-pasteurized	1 month	Do not freeze
Whipped, sweetened	1 day	1–2 months
Aerosol can, real whipped cream	3–4 weeks	Do not freeze
Aerosol can, non-dairy topping	3 months	Do not freeze
Cream, half-and-half	3–4 days	4 months
Dips, sour cream based	2 weeks	Do not freeze
Egg substitutes, liquid	10 days unopened, 3 days opened	Do not freeze
Eggs, in shell	3–5 weeks	Do not freeze
Raw whites, yolks*	2–4 days	12 months
Hard cooked	1 week	Doesn't freeze well
Kefir (fermented milk)	1 week after date; opened 1–2 days	Do not freeze
Margarine	6 months	12 months
Milk, plain or flavoured	1 week	3 months
Pudding	Package date; 2 days after opening	Do not freeze
Sour cream	7–21 days	Doesn't freeze well
Yogurt	7–14 days	1–2 months

*When freezing egg yolks, beat in either ⅛ teaspoon salt or 1½ teaspoons sugar or golden/light corn syrup per 4 egg yolks.

Product	Refrigerated	Frozen
Dough		
Tube cans of dough (biscuits, rolls, pizza dough, etc.)	'Use-by' date	Do not freeze
Ready-to-bake pie crust	'Use-by' date	2 months
Cookie dough	'Use-by' date, unopened or opened	2 months
Fish		
Lean fish (cod, flounder, haddock, halibut, sole, etc.)	1–2 days	6–8 months
Lean fish (pollock, ocean perch, rockfish, sea trout, etc.)	1–2 days	4 months
Fatty fish (bluefish, mackerel, salmon, tuna, etc.)	1–2 days	2–3 months
Caviar, fresh, in jar	1–4 weeks; 2 days open	Doesn't freeze well
Cooked fish, all	3–4 days	1–2 months
Surimi seafood	3–4 days or package date	9 months

Product	Refrigerated	Frozen
Shellfish		
Prawns/shrimp, scallops, crayfish, squid	1–2 days	3–6 months
Shucked clams, mussels and oysters	1–2 days	3–4 months
Crab meat, fresh	1–2 days	4 months
Crab meat, pasteurized	6 months unopened; 3–5 days opened	4 months
Crab legs, king, dungeness, snow	5 days	9–12 months
Live clams, mussels, crab and oysters	1–2 days	2–3 months
Live lobsters	1–2 days	2–3 months
Lobster tails	1–2 days	6 months
Cooked shellfish, all	3–4 days	3 months
Smoked fish		
Herring	3–4 days	2 months
Salmon, whitefish, cold-smoked	5–8 days	2 months
Salmon, whitefish, hot smoked	14 days or date on vacuum pkg	6 months in vacuum pkg
Meat, fresh		
Beef, lamb, pork or veal chops, steaks, roasts	3–5 days	4–12 months
Minced/ground meat	1–2 days	3–4 months
Variety meats (liver, tongue, chitterlings, etc.)	1–2 days	3–4 months
Cooked meats (after home cooking)	3–4 days	2–3 months
Meat, smoked or processed		
Bacon	1 week	1 month
Corned beef, in pouch with pickling juices	5–7 days	1 month
Ham, canned ('keep refrigerated' label)	6–9 months	Do not freeze
Ham, fully cooked, whole	1 week	1–2 months
Ham, fully cooked, slices or half	3–4 days	1–2 months
Ham, cook before eating	1 week	1–2 months
Hot dogs, sealed in package	2 weeks	1–2 months
Hot dogs, after opening	1 week	1–2 months
Lunch meats, sealed in package	2 weeks	1–2 months
Lunch meats, after opening	3–5 days	1–2 months
Sausage, raw, bulk type	1–2 days	1–2 months
Sausage, smoked links, patties	1 week	1–2 months
Sausage, hard, dry (pepperoni), sliced	2–3 weeks	1–2 months
Pasta, fresh	1–2 days or 'use-by' date on package	2 months
Pesto or salsa	Date on carton; 3 days after opening	1–2 months
Poultry, fresh		
Chicken or turkey, whole	1–2 days	12 months
Chicken or turkey, parts	1–2 days	9 months
Duckling or goose, whole	1–2 days	6 months
Giblets	1–2 days	3–4 months
Poultry, cooked or processed		
Chicken nuggets, patties	1–2 days	1–3 months
Cooked poultry dishes	3–4 days	4–6 months

Product	Refrigerated	Frozen
Fried chicken	3–4 days	4 months
Lunch meats, sealed in package	2 weeks	1–2 months
Lunch meats, after opening	3–5 days	1–2 months
Minced/ground turkey or chicken	1–2 days	3–4 months
Pieces covered with broth or gravy	1–2 days	6 months
Rotisserie chicken	3–4 days	4 months

Soy products

Soy or rice beverage, refrigerated	7–10 days	Do not freeze
Tofu	1 week or package date	5 months
Miso	3 months	Do not freeze

FRESH FRUITS AND VEGETABLES

Fruits	Shelf	Refrigerator	Frozen
Apples	1–2 days	3 weeks	Cooked, 8 months
Apricots	Until ripe	2–3 days	Do not freeze
Avocados	Until ripe	3–4 days	Do not freeze
Bananas	Until ripe	2 days, skin will blacken	Whole peeled, 1 month
Berries, cherries		1–2 days	4 months
Citrus fruit	10 days	1–2 weeks	Do not freeze
Coconuts, fresh	1 week	2–3 weeks	Shredded, 6 months
Grapes	1 day	1 week	Whole, 1 month
Kiwi fruit	Until ripe	3–4 days	Do not freeze
Melons	1–2 days	3–4 days	Balls, 1 month
Papaya, mango	3–5 days	1 week	Do not freeze
Peaches, nectarines	Until ripe	3–4 days	Sliced, lemon juice and sugar, 2 months
Pears, plums	3–5 days	3–4 days	Do not freeze

Vegetables	Shelf	Refrigerator	Frozen*
Artichokes, whole	1–2 days	1–2 weeks	Do not freeze
Asparagus		3–4 days	8 months
Aubergine/eggplant	1 day	3–4 days	6–8 months
Beans, green or wax		3–4 days	8 months
Beetroot/beets	1 day	7–10 days	6–8 months
Broccoli, raab, rapini		3–5 days	10–12 months
Brussels sprouts		3–5 days	10–12 months
Cauliflower		3–5 days	10–12 months
Cabbage		1–2 weeks	10–12 months
Carrots, parsnips		3 weeks	10–12 months
Celery		1–2 weeks	10–12 months
Corn on the cob		1–2 days	8 months
Cucumbers		4–5 days	Do not freeze
Garlic	1 month	1–2 weeks	1 month
Ginger root	1–2 days	1–2 weeks	1 month
Greens		1–2 days	10–12 months
Herbs, fresh		7–10 days	1–2 months

Vegetables	Shelf	Refrigerator	Frozen
Leeks		1–2 weeks	10–12 months
Lettuce, iceberg		1–2 weeks	Do not freeze
Lettuce, leaf		3–7 days	Do not freeze
Mushrooms		2–3 days	10–12 months
Okra/ladies' fingers		2–3 days	10–12 months
Onions, dry	2–3 weeks	2 months	10–12 months
Spring/scallions or green		1–2 weeks	10–12 months
Pak choi/bok choy		2–3 days	10–12 months
Parsley, coriander/cilantro		1 week	1–2 months
Peppers, bell or chilli/chile		4–5 days	6–8 months
Potatoes	1–2 months	1–2 weeks	Cooked & mashed, 10–12 months
Radishes		10–14 days	Do not freeze
Spinach		1–2 days	10–12 months
Squash, Summer		4–5 days	10–12 months
Winter	1 week	2 weeks	10–12months
Swede/rutabagas	1 week	2 weeks	8–10 months
Turnips		2 weeks	8–10 months
Tomatoes	Until ripe	2–3 days	2 months

*It is recommended to blanch (partially cook) or cook vegetables before freezing.

FOODS PURCHASED FROZEN

Frozen items	Freezer	Refrigerator after thawing
Bagels	2 months	1–2 weeks
Bread dough, commercial	'Use-by' date	After baking, 4–7 days
Burritos, sandwiches	2 months	3–4 days
Egg substitutes	12 months	Date on carton
Fish, breaded	3–6 months	Do not defrost; cook frozen
Fish, raw	6 months	1–2 days
Fruit (berries, melons, etc.)	4–6 months	4–5 days
Guacamole	3–4 months	3–4 days
Ice cream	2–4 months	
Juice concentrates	6–12 months	7–10 days
Lobster tails	3 months	2 days
Pancakes, waffles	2 months	3–4 days
Ready-prepared meals/TV dinners, entrées, breakfast	3 months	Do not defrost; cook frozen
Sausages, uncooked	1–2 months	1–2 days
Pre-cooked	1–2 months	1 week
Sherbet, sorbet	2–4 months	
Shrimp, shellfish	12 months	1–2 days
Soy crumbles and hotdogs	9 months	3–4 days
Soy meat substitutes	12–18 months	3–4 days
Tempeh	12 months	1–2 weeks
Topping, whipped	6 months	2 weeks
Vegetables	8 months	3–4 days

Deli foods	Refrigerator	Frozen
Main dishes or meals, hot or refrigerated	3–4 days	2–3 months
Meats covered with gravy or broth	1–2 days	6 months
Commercial brand vacuum-packed meal/USDA seal	2 weeks	Does not freeze well
Chicken, rotisserie or fired	3–4 days	4 months
Luncheon meats, store-sliced	3–5 days	1–2 months
Paté	1–2 days	1–2 months
Cheese, store-sliced, hard cheese (Cheddar, Swiss, etc.)	3–4 weeks	6 months
Cheese, soft (brie, bel paese, goat cheese, mozzarella, etc.)	1 week	6 months
Salads containing meat, fish, poultry or eggs	3–4 days	Don't freeze
Salads, vegetable	3–5 days	Don't freeze
Side dishes (cooked vegetables, rice, potatoes etc.)	3–4 days	1–2 months
Olives	2 weeks	Don't freeze
Pudding	'Use-by' date; 2 days after opening	Don't freeze
Fruit, cut	'Use-by' date; 4 days after opening	Don't freeze
Cheesecake	1 week	2–3 months

SHELF-STABLE FOODS

Shelf stable food	Unopened in pantry	Refrigerator after opening	In pantry after opening
Baby food, jars or cans			
Fruits and vegetables	"Use-by" date	2–3 days	
Meats and eggs	"Use-by" date	1 day	
Cereal, dry mixes	"Use-by" date		2 months
Formula	"Use-by" date	1–2 days	
Bacon bits, imitation	4 months	refer to jar	4 months
Beans, dried	12 months		12 months
Canned goods, low acid	2–5 years	3–4 days	
(meat, poultry, fish, gravy, stew, soups, beans, carrots, corn, pasta, peas, potatoes, spinach, etc.)			
Canned goods, high acid	12–18 months	5–7 days	
(juices, fruit, pickles, sauerkraut, tomato soup, and foods in vinegar-based sauce, etc.)			
Cereal, ready-to-eat	6–12 months		3 months
Cook before eating	12 months		6–12 months
(e.g. oatmeal)			
Coffee, whole beans	1–3 weeks	3–4 months frozen, 2 weeks refrigerated	1 week
Non-vacuum bag, ground	2 years	3–4 months frozen, 2 weeks refrigerated	1 week
Instant, jars & tins	12 months	3–4 months frozen, 2 weeks refrigerated	2–3 months

Baking ingredients

Baking powder	6 months		3 months
Bicarbonate of soda/ baking soda	18 months		6 months
Biscuit or pancake mix	15 months		'Use-by' date
Cake, brownie, bread mixes	12–18 months		'Use-by' date

Shelf stable food	Unopened in pantry	Refrigerator after opening	In pantry after opening
Cornstarch/cornmeal (regular, degerminated)	6–12 months	12 months	
Stoneground or blue	1 month	2–3 months	
Cornflour/cornstarch	18 months		18 months
Flour, white	6–12 months		6–8 months
Wholemeal/whole wheat	1 month	6–8 months	
Frosting, canned	10 months	1 week	3 months
Frosting mixes	12 months		3 months
Chocolate, plain/bittersweet	18–24 months		1 year
milk/semi-sweet	18–24 months		1 year
Chocolate syrup	2 years	6 months	
Cocoa and cocoa mixes	Indefinitely		1 year

Condiments

	Unopened in pantry	Refrigerator after opening	In pantry after opening
Barbecue sauce, bottled	12 months	4 months	1 month
Ketchup or cocktail sauce	12 months	6 months	1 month
Chutney	12 months	1–2 months	
Horseradish, in jar	12 months	3–4 months	
Mayonnaise, commercial	2–3 months	2 months	
Mustard	12 months	12 months	1 month
Olives, black and green	12–18 months	2 weeks	
Pickles	12 months	1–2 weeks	
Salad dressing, commercial	10–12 months	3 months	
Salsa, picante and taco sauces	12 months	1 month	
Cookies, packaged	2 months	8–12 months frozen	4 weeks
Crackers	8 months	Freeze or refrigerate, 3–4 months	1 month
Diet powder mixes	6 months		3 months
Extracts, vanilla, lemon, etc.	3 years		1 year
Fruits, dried	6 months	6 months	1 month
Garlic, chopped	18 months	Refrigerate, 'use-by' date on jar	
Commercial jars	8 months	Refrigerate, 'use-by' date on jar	
Gelatin, flavoured	18 months		Use all or reseal for 3–4 months
Unflavoured	3 years		Use all or reseal for 3–4 months
Gravy, jars and cans	2–5 years	1–2 days	Use entire can
Dry gravy mixes	2 years	1–2 days	Mix entire packet
Herbs, dried	1–2 years		Cool, dark place 1 year
Honey	12 months		12 months
Jams, jellies, preserves	12 months	6 months	
Jerky, commercially dried	12 months	2–3 months	
Jerky, homemade		1–2 months	1–2 months
Juice, boxes	4–6 months	8–12 days	
Lentils, dried	12 months		12 months
Marshmallows	2–4 months		1 month
Milk, canned evaporated	12 months	4–5 days	
Molasses	12 months		6 months

Shelf stable food	Unopened in pantry	Refrigerator after opening	In pantry after opening
Mushrooms, dried	6 months		3 months
Oils, olive or vegetable	6 months	4 months	1–3 months
Nut oils	6 months		
Vegetable oil sprays	2 years		1 year
Nuts, jars or cans	12 months	Refrigerate 4–6 months, Freeze 9–12 months	1 month
Pasta, dry, without eggs	2 years		1 year
Dry egg noodles	2 years		1–2 months
Peanut butter, commercial	6–9 months		2–3 months
Peas, dried split	12 months		12 months
Pectin	'Use-by' date		1 month
Popcorn, dry kernels in jar	2 years		1 year
Commercially popped in bags	2–3 months		1–2 weeks
Microwave packets	12 months		1–2 days popped
Potato chips	2 months		1–2 weeks
Potatoes, instant	6–12 months		6–12 months
Pudding mixes	12 months		3–4 months
Rice, white or wild	2 years	6 months	1 year
Brown	1 year	6 months	1 year
Flavoured or herb mix	6 months	6 months	Use all
Sauce mixes, non-dairy (spaghetti, taco, etc.)	2 years		Use entire amount
cream sauces, milk solids	1 year		
Shortening, solid	8 months		3 months
Soda such as carbonated cola drinks, mixers			
Diet sodas, bottles/cans	3 months after date	2–3 days	1 week
Regular sodas, bottles	3 months after date	2–3 days	2 weeks
Regular sodas, cans	9 months after date		
Soup mixes, dry bouillon	12 months		12 months
Soy products			
Soy or rice beverage (shelf stable)	3 months or "use-by" date	7–10 days	
Soy beverage powders	6 months		3–4 months
Soy flour, de-fatted, low fat	1 year		1 year
Soy flour, full-fat	2 months	6 months	
Textured soy protein (TSP)	2 years		3–4 months
Re-hydrated TSP	3–4 months	3–4 days	
Spaghetti sauce in jars	18 months	4 days	
Spices, whole	2–4 years total		Included in total
Ground	2–3 years total		Included in total
Paprika, red pepper	2 years total	Store in refrigerator	Included in total
Chili powder	2 years total	Store in refrigerator	Included in total
Sugar, brown	4 months		Sugar never spoils
Granulated	2 years		
Confectioners	18 months		
Sugar substitutes	2 years		
Syrup, pancake	12 months		12 months
Genuine or real maple	12 months	12 months	
Tapioca	12 months		12 months

Shelf stable food	Unopened in pantry	Refrigerator after opening	In pantry after opening
Tea bags	18 months		12 months
Loose leaf	2 years		6–12 months
Instant	3 years		6–12 months
Toaster pastries, fruit filled	6 months		Keep foil packets sealed
Non-fruit fillings	9 months		Keep foil packets sealed
Tomatoes, sun-dried			
Packed in oil	12 months	6–12 months	3–6 months
Packed in cellophane	9 months	6–12 months	3–6 months
Vinegar	2 years		12 months
Yeast, dry, packets and jars	'Use-by' date	Refrigerate open jars	
Water, bottled	1–2 years		3 months
Worcestershire sauce	1 year		1 year

Bakery items	Shelf	Refrigerator	Freezer
Bread, commercial*	2–4 days	7–14 days	3 months
Bread, flat (tortillas, pita)	2–4 days	4–7 days	4 months
Cakes, Angel food**	1–2 days	1 week	2 months
Chiffon, sponge	1–2 days	1 week	2 months
Chocolate	1–2 days	1 week	4 months
Fruit cake	1 month	6 months	12 months
Made from mix	3–4 days	1 week	4 months
Pound cake	3–4 days	1 week	6 months
Cheesecake		1 week	2–3 months
Cookies, bakery or homemade	2–3 weeks	2 months	8–12 months
Croissants, butter	1 day	1 week	2 months
Doughnuts, glazed or cake	1–2 days	1 week	1 month
Dairy cream filled		3–4 days	
Eclairs/cream puffs, dairy cream filled		3–4 days	
Muffins	1–2 days	1 week	2 months
Pastries, Danish	1–2 days	1 week	2 months
Pies, Cream		3–4 days	
Chiffon		1–2 days	
Fruit	1–2 days	1 week	8 months
Mincemeat	2 hours	1 week	8 months
Pecan	2 hours	3–4 days	1–2 months
Pumpkin	2 hours	3–4 days	1–2 months
Quiche	2 hours	3–4 days	2 months
Rolls, Yeast	3–4 days	1 week	2 months
Yeast, partially baked	Package date	1 week	2 months
Filled, meat or vegetables	2 hours	3–4 days	2 months

*Any breads containing meat, hard-boiled/hard-cooked eggs, custard filling or other perishable ingredients must be refrigerated within two hours.

**Refrigerate any cake with frosting made of dairy products or eggs.

Food safety

Improper handling of food in the home causes most food-borne illness. Micro-organisms multiply rapidly at temperatures between 4°C (40°F) and 72°C (140°F), and most can't be seen, smelled or tasted. Always make sure your hands are immaculately clean before handling food and that your counter, utensils, chopping blocks, pots and all other cooking paraphernalia are spotless, too.

SAFETY BASICS

• Keep your hands and your kitchen immaculate at all times.

• Observe proper cooking temperatures for your food.

• Plan your meals so that you serve them hot – 72°C (140°F) or hotter – or cold at 4°C (40°F) or colder. Do not leave them on countertops, which makes them less safe to consume. Warm air in the kitchen will promote bacterial growth within minutes of cooking. Meals need to be eaten right away, or chilled then refrigerated.

• Place leftovers in the refrigerator within 2 hours of finishing the meal.

• Refrigerate or freeze food quickly and in small quantities.

• Leftovers should be properly reheated so their internal temperature is 72°C (140°F) or higher.

• Never prepare leftovers and uncooked food together. Always cook them separately.

• When food is left over, discard the original container or put it in the dishwasher. Always store leftover food in a clean container.

• Never thaw foods in the kitchen sink or at room temperature. Ideally this should be done in the microwave,

in the refrigerator, or in ice water.

• Always rinse your fruits and vegetables thoroughly before cooking, no matter how shiny and polished-looking they are. Spray them with germ-free solution for rinsing vegetables, which can be purchased at specialist food stores for this purpose.

• Any mould on hard cheese, fruit, and so on can be sliced off, but be sure to chop off extra to be on the safe side. Mould is insidious, dangerous and the residue odour clings.

• Mushy vegetables, fruit, cottage cheese and any other soft food must be tossed out as a whole if you notice any mould. Simply removing the 'bad' part is not enough.

• Be sure to dry salad after thorough washing to prevent sogginess – you can use a salad spinner to do this. Soggy food becomes mouldy fast. Don't serve day-old prepared salad.

• Make sure any cans and bottles you take from the pantry are completely dust-free before opening them, so always wash them first.

• Buy the smallest waste bin/trash can available and line it with a small plastic garbage bag. Keep it at the side of your sink for all the 'waste' from your daily food preparation. After every meal, remove and toss out the disposable bag and replace it with a fresh one.

• After chopping or cooking, clean all kitchen surfaces and chopping blocks with hot water and detergent. Most utensils, except wood-handled ones, can be cleaned in the dishwasher.

• Check out new products: square cutting sheets, for example, are great for mopping up juices, blood and grease from chicken and meat roasts, and also protect your cutting board.

PACKET DATES

'Sell-by' date: buy the product before this date expires. The product is usually safe to use for 1 week past the date – except for eggs, milk and cottage cheese – if transported and stored in a proper manner. Sell-by dates can be found on meats, processed cheeses and orange juice from concentrate in cartons.

Expiration or 'use-by' date: refers to the last date recommended by the manufacturer for use of the product. Don't ever ignore it.

Freshness or 'best-if-used-by' date: recommended for best flavour and quality. Bakery products, boxed cereals and some pre-cut vegetables have this label.

Kitchen equipment

Whether you're a young bachelor or gourmet chef, a mother of five, or a new bride, your kitchen needs utensils. Which will suit your purpose? A wide variety exists at your disposal from the most basic to the most sophisticated. A kitchen is as efficient as the equipment it holds.

THE BASIC KITCHEN

Some basic utensils and culinary tools are essential, even if you hardly ever cook at home. If you have even the most rudimentary of kitchens, you will be able to whip up very simple meals at a moment's notice. This is as basic as it gets!

Utensils

2 wooden spoons
1 large metal spoon
1 large slotted metal spoon
1 pair tongs
1 paring or utility knife
1 serrated knife
1 large chopping knife
1 pair kitchen scissors
1 sharpening steel
Heatproof/Pyrex jug/pitcher
Measuring cups
1 thermometer, instant-read
1 grater
1 colander
salt and pepper mills
2 chopping blocks
1 can opener
1 corkscrew
1 strainer, fine mesh
1 cafetière and/or tea infuser

Pots and pans

3 saucepans – small, medium
    and large, with lids
1 large non-stick frying pan/
    skillet
1 heavy shallow pan with
    ovenproof handles

Baking pans

1 non-stick roasting pan
1 non-stick baking sheet

Utility drawer

aluminium foil
clingfilm/plastic wrap
medium freezer bags
oven gloves

Washing-up/dishwashing

1 washing-up bowl/
    dishwashing tub
1 draining rack/mat
2 nylon scrapers (for non-
    stick surfaces and enamel)
2 wire brushes (for pots
    and pans)
2 bottle brushes
5 kitchen cloths
rubber gloves

THE DREAM KITCHEN

When you've finally got the basics down, it's time to invest in a kitchen that has more elaborate, but still important equipment. This is when your kitchen can truly shine – where you can create beautiful culinary dishes, mouthwatering desserts and experiment in ethnic cuisine. For this, you will need an array of utensils not needed in a truly basic kitchen.

Utensils

1 chef's knife
1 carving knife and/or boning knife
2 paring knives
2 scoops of different sizes
2 forks – 1 large and 1 small
2–3 plastic chopping blocks (assorted sizes)
4 pairs of chopsticks (non-disposable)
4 metal skewers
6 corn-on-the-cob holders
8 steak knives
bottle opener
citrus-fruit juicer
funnel
kitchen shears (sharpen when dull)
meshed spoon for deep-frying
pestle and mortar
olive oil drizzler
pancake turners
plastic Japanese tongs for stir-fry
plastic spatula or scraper
potato masher
soup ladle
strainers, large and small
vegetable scrubbing brush
vegetable peeler
wire whisk

Baking pans

1 Bundt cake pan
2 20-cm/8-in. round non-stick cake pans
2 23-cm/9-in. round non-stick cake pans
2 springform cake pans (23-cm/9-in. and 25-cm/10-in.)
4 loaf pans (2 450-g/1-lb. pans, 2 675-g/1½-lb pans)
2 square cake pans
12-hole non-stick muffin pan
2 large cookie sheets
6 ramekins
3 glass bowls: small, medium and large
rolling pin
fine, mesh sieve/strainer

Essential pots and pans

20–25-cm/8–10-in. skillet: cast-iron and non-stick
double-boiler
Dutch oven
frying pan/sauté pan
steamer
large stockpot
stove-top griddle/grill pan
tea kettle
wok

Equipment

10 tight-lidded plastic refrigerator/freezer storage tubs (all sizes)
6 storage jars, light-proof and airtight
glass measuring cup, 1 litre/quart or ½ litre/1 pint
glass measuring cup, 250-ml/1-cup size
dry measuring cups
2 sets of measuring spoons
meat thermometer
refrigerator/freezer thermometers
oven thermometer (absolutely essential!)
12-hour kitchen timer

Small appliances

coffee grinder
coffee maker/cappuccino maker
electric mixer
food processor or blender
grinder or food mill; they also grind spices
hand-held electric blender
juicer
electric kettle
microwave
toaster or toaster oven

Utility drawer

baking parchment
writing pad (adhesive or magnetized for refrigerator)
pens and pencils
household appliance manuals
contact details for all service personnel

Linen

tablecloths and napkins for as many days per week used
1 dozen kitchen cloths (3–4 linen ones for glass, crystal and good china)
1 dozen dishcloths
4 potholders (use more if these get soiled during the week)
2–3 pieces of cheesecloth for cooking, straining
2–3 aprons (again, change if you need more)

*Keep a ragbag. Add to it from old sheets, your or your partner's used undershirts, and other used cotton discards. Cut into strips and squares for easy use.

Entertaining basics

Your storecupboard is well stocked and your refrigerator is brimming full of sumptuous, fresh produce. The afternoon has been spent gleaning all the old and new recipes, culling from them your favourite dishes and your guests are arriving soon. But, before all else, you need to know the basics of a finely set table. A table set with row upon row of eating tools can seem daunting but this need not be the case. Provided the table is laid correctly and you follow the simple rule of using the outermost utensil or utensils first, you can't go wrong.

TABLE-SETTING BASICS

• Make sure your tableware is completely clean and polished.

• Set dishes and cutlery/flatware evenly and geometrically, so everyone's setting is the same.

• Put the cutlery/flatware face up.

• Knives and spoons go to the right of the plate. The spoon goes to the right of the knife and the knife edge faces toward the plate.

• Forks go to the left of the plate.

• Dessert utensils may be placed above the dinner plate, parallel to the edge of the table.

• The teaspoon for coffee or tea is placed on the saucer.

• The butter knife is placed on the bread plate.

• Napkins go to the left of the forks or on the centre of the bread plate.

• Water glasses go to the right, above the dinner plate.

• Wine glasses go to the right below the water glass. If both red and white wine are to be served, the white wine glass goes closer to the cutlery.

• Bread plates go to the left, above the dinner plate.

• When salad is eaten with the main course, its dish is placed to the left of the dinner plate.

BASIC CHINA, GLASSWARE AND TABLEWARE SET TO SERVE EIGHT GUESTS

China
Dinner plate
Salad plate
Cup and saucer
Cereal bowl
Dessert plate
Demitasse
Bread plate

Serving dishes
Platter, large
Platter, small
Serving bowls, 3 sizes
Sauce or gravy boat
Glass or crystal
 water cruet
Creamer
Sugar bowl
Teapot and coffee pot
Small dishes, variety

Serving peices
Ladle, large
Ladle, small
Spoon, sugar tongs
Salad servers

Large three-pronged
 fork
Serving spoons

Cutlery
Dinner fork
Salad fork
Knife
Steak knife
Teaspoon
Soup spoon
Dessert spoon
 and/or fork
Butter knife

Drinks
8 water goblets
8 juice glasses
Red wine glasses
White wine glasses
Highball glasses
Brandy snifters
Champagne flutes
Martini glasses
Margarita glasses
Liqueur glasses

International informal

The most common setting for an informal Western meal positions the dinner knife to the right of the dinner plate with the soup spoon to the right of the knife. The dinner fork is to the left of the plate with the napkin to the left of the fork. The dessert fork and spoon are laid horizontally above the plate, the fork first with the handle to the left, and the spoon above it with the handle to the right. The glasses go to the right, above the dinner plate, with the white wine glass above the knife, the red wine glass above it and to the left, and the water glass left of that.

UK formal

A formal meal provides an opportunity to use lots of china and silverware. If you have a large dining table, make full use of the space by laying the dessert spoon and fork inside the dinner knife and fork, and by including a butter plate to the left of the setting.

US formal

This setting is for a formal three-course meal with a fish appetizer. A butter knife is optional and would be laid on the bread plate. When eating the main course, the dinner fork is transferred to the right hand for each bite, and back to the left hand when the knife is needed for cutting. Dessert utensils can also be laid across the top of the setting or brought in when dessert is served. It is not necessary to use both spoon and fork, but may be easier.

French formal

French settings differ from American and British in a number of ways. Bread plates and butter knives are not used; bread is laid directly on the table, and butter is not served. Forks and spoons rest face down, and a tablespoon is used for soup in favor of the more rounded soup spoon. A knife rest is provided so the dinner knife can be laid back on the table, ready to be used for the cheese course, before dessert is served.

Resources

UK RESOURCES

John Lewis
03456 049 049 (UK)
+44 (0)1698 54 54 54 (international)
www.johnlewis.com
Tools, cleaning products, household linen, furniture and kitchenware.

Labour and Wait
+44 (0)20 7729 6253
www.labourandwait.co.uk
Traditional tools and houseware.

Lakeland
+44 (0)1539 488100
www.lakeland.co.uk
Household tools, laundry and kitchenware by mail order.

Manufactum Ltd.
+44 (0)800 096 0938
www.manufactum.co.uk
Quality tools and kitchenware.

Selfridges
0800 123 400 (UK)
+44 (0)113 369 8040 (international)
www.selfridges.com
Housework tools as well as lighting and kitchenware.

Cleaning products and cleansers

Challs International Ltd.
+44 (0)870 603 0420
www.challs.com
Cleaning products for every area of your home, available to buy online.

Healthier Solutions
+44 (0)1785 878 167
www.healthiersolutions.co.uk
Environmentally friendly products.

Vale Mill (Rochdale) Ltd.
+ 44 (0)1706 353 535
www.minky.com
Supplier of a wide range of cloths for cleaning specific materials.

Floors, walls and surfaces

CD (UK) Ltd.
+44 (0)113 201 2240
www.cdukltd.co.uk
Supplier and distributor of Corian®.

Crucial Trading Ltd.
+44 (0)1562 743 747
www.crucial-trading.com
Carpets and rugs including natural fibres: sisal, coir, rush, jute and others.

Dalsouple
+44 (0)1278 727 777 (for stockists)
www.dalsouple.com
Rubber flooring in many colours.

The Delabole Slate Company
+44 (0)1840 212242
www.delaboleslate.com
Riven slate tiles or slate slabs for flooring, paving, sills and fireplaces.

Leather Care Master (UK) Ltd.
+44 (0)1244 888 658
www.leathermasteruk.com
Care and repair products for leather.

Original Tile Company
+44 (0)131 225 7356
www.originaltilecompany.co.uk
Terracotta, limestone, slate and marble, Victorian and Morocccan encaustic tiles.

Paris Ceramics
+44 (0)20 7371 7778
www.parisceramics.com
Limestone and terracotta flooring, mosaics and decorative tiles.

Tarkett Ltd.
+44 (0)1622 854000
www.tarkett.co.uk
Vinyl flooring.

Kitchens

The Cooks Kitchen
+44 (0)1275 842 883
www.thecookskitchen.com
Cookware, tools and cleaning products.

Dawson's Department Store
+44 (0)1200 421 010
www.dawsonsdepartmentstore.co.uk
Discounted cookware.

Divertimenti
+44 (0)330 333 0351
www.divertimenti.co.uk
Cookware, tableware and storage.

Habitat
+44 (0)344 499 1111 (store locator)
+44 (0)344 499 4686

www.habitat.net
Home accessories and furniture.

Heal's
+44 (0)20 7896 7451
www.heals.co.uk
Contemporary kitchenware, furniture and storage.

Bathrooms

Bathroom Renovations Ltd.
+44 (0)20 8894 6464
www.bathrenovationltd.co.uk
Re-enamelling service for baths.

Inter-Bath Restoration Services
+44 (0)800 026 0070
Re-enamelling service for baths.

Laundry

**Home Laundering
Consultative Council**
+44 (0)20 7843 9460
www.care-labelling.co.uk
Information on how best to wash, dry or clean clothes.

Bedding and household linen

Acton and Acton Ltd.
+44 (0)1706 642 361
www.actonandactonltd.co.uk
Special-sized bedding specialists.

The Eiderdown Studio
+44 (0)1395 271147
Recovers worn duvets.

Givan's
+44 (0)1733 562 300
www.givans.co.uk
Luxury supplier of Irish linen.

Jeeves of Belgravia
+44 (0)20 8809 3232
www.jeevesofbelgravia.co.uk
Vacuum packing service.

Keys of Clacton
+44 (0)1255 432 518
www.bedlinencentre.co.uk
Special-sized bedding.

Marks & Spencer
0333 014 8000 (UK)
+44 (0)208 090 9564 (international)
www.marksandspencer.com
Good-quality towels and kitchenware.

Storage

The Conran Shop
+44 (0)20 7403 8899
www.conran.com
Contemporary accessories.

Conservation by Design
+44 (0)1234 846 300
www.conservation-by-design.co.uk
*Acid-free tissue for storing all sorts
of household items.*

The Holding Company
+44 (0)20 8445 2888
www.theholdingcompany.co.uk
*A range of innovative storage solutions
for every room in the home.*

Ikea
+44 (0)20 3645 0000
www.ikea.com
*Good value kitchen units, furniture
and storage for allaround the home.*

Muji
www.muji.eu
*Steel and cardboard modular shelving,
plus cardboard, acrylic, fabric and
polypropylene storage boxes.*

Food

Chilled Food Association
www.chilledfood.org
*Promotes best hygienic practice
standards in the production of retailed
chilled prepared food.*

**Food Storage &
Distribution Federation**
www.fsdf.org.uk
*An trade organization for companies
involved in or associated with the
UK food and drink storage and
distribution industry.*

Lighting

Bella Figura
+44 (0)20 7376 4564 (showroom)
and +44 (0)1394 461 111 (warehouse
and factory outlet)
www.bella-figura.com
*Manufacturers of decorative lighting
including wall and table lamps.*

Christopher Wray Lighting
+44 (0)20 7013 0180
www.christopherwray.com

*Over 4,000 lights, light fittings
and lighting accessories.*

Stiffkey Lamp Shop
+44 (0)1328 820 907
enquiries@stiffkeylampshop.com
www.stiffkeylampshop.com
*Original Victorian and Edwardian
lights, wall brackets and oil lamps.*

Useful Organizations

Allergy UK
+44 (0)1322 619 898
www.allergyuk.org

**Association of British
Pewter Craftsmen**
www.britishpewter.co.uk

Association of Master Upholsterers
+44 (0)1494 569 120
www.upholsterers.co.uk

Asthma UK
+44 (0)20 7786 4900
www.asthma.org.uk

Bathroom Manufacturers' Association
+44 (0)1782 631 619
www.bathroom-association.org

**British Blind and Shutter
Association (BBSA)**
+44 (0)1449 780 444
www.bbsa.org.uk

**British Carpet
Manufacturers' Association**
+44 (0)1562 755 568
www.carpetfoundation.com

**British Cutlery and
Silverware Association**
+44 (0)114 266 3084

**British Furniture Restorers'
Association**
+44 (0)1939 210 826
www.bafra.org.uk

**British Pest Control Association
(BPCA)**
+44 (0)1332 294 288
www.bpca.org.uk

The Building Centre
+44 (0)20 7692 4000
www.buildingcentre.co.uk

**Building & Engineering Services
Association**
+44 (0)20 7313 4900
www.b-es.org

**Chartered Institute of Plumbing and
Heating Engineering (CIPHE)**
+44 (0)1708 472 791
www.ciphe.org.uk

Cork Industry Federation
+44 (0)7814 919 112
www.cork-products.co.uk

Glass and Glazing Federation (GGF)
+44 (0)20 7939 9101
www.ggf.org.uk

Guild of Master Craftsmen
+44 (0)1273 477 374
www.thegmcgroup.com

**The Kitchen Bathroom Bedroom
Specialists Association (KBSA)**
+44 (0)1623 818 808
www.kbsa.co.uk

**National Association of
Chimney Sweeps (NACS)**
+44 (0)1785 811 732
www.nacs.org.uk

National Bed Federation
+44 (0)1756 799 950
www.bedfed.org.uk

**National Carpet Cleaners'
Association Ltd. (NCCA)**
+44 (0)116 271 9550
www.ncca.co.uk

Stone Federation of Great Britain
+44 (0)1303 856 123
www.stonefed.org.uk

Trading Standards
+44 (0)3454 04 05 06
www.tradingstandards.gov.uk

Textile Services Association (TSA)
+44 (0)20 7843 9490
www.tsa-uk.org

Vitreous Enamel Association (VEA)
+44 (0)1543 450 596
www.vea.org.uk

US RESOURCES

Cleaning products and cleansers

Caldrea Aromatherapeutic Living
www.caldrea.com
Eco-friendly cleaning products.

Casabella
www.casabella.com
Cleaning tools and products for every aspect of the home.

Earth Friendly Products
www.ecos.com
Eco-friendly cleaning products.

Naturally Yours
www.naturallyyoursclean.com
Eco-safe cleaning product line.

Restoration Hardware
www.restorationhardware.com
High-end home store with own-brand cleaning products, home furnishings, lighting and accessories.

Safe Home Products
www.safehomeproducts.com
Non-toxic cleaning products.

Floors, walls and surfaces

American Hardwoods
www.hardwood.org
Information on choosing, sourcing and maintaining American hardwood flooring and other surfaces.

Ancor Granite Tile Inc.
www.ancor.ca
Granite supplier.

Anne Sacks Tile & Stone
www.annsacks.com
Limestone, terra-cotta, marble, mosaics, handcrafted tile.

Armstrong World Industries, Inc.
www.armstrong.com
Vinyl and laminate flooring.

Formica Corporation
www.formica.com
Laminate furniture and surfaces.

Foro Marble Company Inc.
www.foromarblecompany.com
Flooring and counters.

Innovations in Wallcoverings, Inc.
www.innovationsusa.com
Wallpaper.

Linoleum City
www.linoleumcity.com
Selection of linoleum.

Marazzi USA
www.marazziusa.com
Glazed floor and wall tiles.

Paris Ceramics
www.parisceramics.com
Ceramic tile supplier.

SILESTONE®
www.silestoneusa.com
Stone supplier.

Stone Care International Inc.
www.stonecare.com
Sealing, cleaning, polishing products for stone surfaces.

Walker Zanger
www.walkerzanger.com
Stone and tile supplier.

Kitchens

Better Homes & Gardens
www.bhg.com
Magazine for house and home.

Cooking.com®
www.cooking.com
Bakeware, cookware, food storage, and tableware.

The Cooks Kitchen
www.thecookskitchen.com
Huge range of kitchenware delivered anywhere in the world.

Corner Hardware
www.cornerhardware.com
Cooking utensils and equipment.

The Chemistry Store
www.chemistrystore.com
Cleaning products for every surface.

DuPont Corian®
www.dupont.com/corian
Non-porous acrylic surface used for counters and sinks.

Franke Inc.
www.franke.com
Stainless steel, granite and titanium sinks and faucets.

Kitchen Collection
www.kitchencollection.com
Kitchen utensils and equipment.

Messermeister
www.messermeister.com
Cutlery, kitchenware and more.

Penzeys Ltd.
www.penzeys.com
Food gift boxes and spice boxes.

Sur La Table
www.surlatable.com
Cooking utensils and equipment.

Williams-Sonoma
www.williams-sonoma.com
Cooking utensils, equipment, fine linens and foodstuffs.

Bathrooms

American Standard
www.americanstandard.com
Tubs, whirlpools, sinks and toilets.

Bed, Bath & Beyond
www.bedbathandbeyond.com
Everything for the bedroom, bathroom and kitchen.

Burgess International Bathroom Fixtures
www.burgessinternational.com
Toilets, bidets, vanities and traditional bathroom furniture.

Cameo Marble
Cultured marble vanity tops, bathtubs and showers.

Custom Marble & Solid Surfaces
www.custommarble.cc
Shower pans, wall surrounds.

Elkay Mfg Co.
www.elkay.com
Sinks, taps/faucets.

Gemini Bath & Kitchen Products
www.geminibkp.com
Showers, sinks.

Kohler Co.
www.kohler.com
Bathroom suites.

MTI Whirlpools
www.mtiwhirlpools.com
Innovative bathroom technology.

Waterworks
www.waterworks.com
Fixtures, fittings, tiles.

Laundry

Gaiam®
www.gaiam.com
Products to purify your home, from organic bed linen to air purifiers.

Ikea
www.ikea.com
Household linens, storage, kitchenware and furniture

Restoration Hardware
www.restorationhardware.com
High-end home store with own-brand laundry products.

Sonin® Water Alarm
www.sonin.com
Water alarms and electronic distance measuring.

Target
www.target.com
Everything, from hampers to retractable clotheslines.

Bedding and household linen

Achoo! Allergy & Air Products
www.achooallergy.com
Mattress and covers for allergy sufferers, as well as air purifiers and special vacuum cleaners.

Garnet Hill
www.garnethill.com
Linens and bedding.

Macy's
www.macys.com
Bedding, furniture etc.

Martex
www.martex.com
Towels and bathsheets.

Pine Cone Hill
www.pineconehill.annieselke.com
Linens and bedding.

Wamsutta®
www.wamsutta.com
Bedding.

Storage

ABC Carpet & Home
www.abchome.com
A fine selections of furniture and storage units.

Biz Rate
www.bizrate.com
Acid-free tissue and storage boxes.

The Container Store
www.thecontainerstore.com
Storage solutions for organizing drawers, pantries, closets.

Crate and Barrel
www.crateandbarrel.com
Good-value furniture, accessories.

Gracious Home
www.gracioushome.com
Everything you need for all rooms.

Rejuvenation®
www.rejuvenation.com
Products for storage organization.

Stacks & Stacks
www.stacksandstacks.com
Products for organizing drawers, pantries, closets, laundry items.

Food

Home Food Safety®
www.homefoodsafety.org
Information regarding food safety in the home.

U.S. Department of Agriculture (USDA) Food Safety and Inspection Service
www.fsis.usda.gov
Food safety cold storage charts.

Useful organizations

Asthma & Allergy Foundations of America
www.aafa.org

The Carpet and Rug Institute
www.carpet-rug.org

Ceramic Tile Institute of America
www.ctioa.org

Chimney Safety Institute of America
www.csia.org

Floor Facts
www.floorfacts.com

Hardwood Manufacturers Association
www.hmamembers.org

Home Ventilating Institute
www.hvi.org

Maple Flooring Manufacturers Association (MFMA)
www.maplefloor.org

Marble Institute of America (MIA)
www.marble-institute.com

National Glass Association
www.glass.org

National Kitchen and Bath Association
www.nkba.org

National Pest Management Association
www.pestworld.org

National Wood Flooring Association (NWFA)
www.nwfa.org

Society of American Silversmiths
www.silversmithing.com

Stone Care International (SCI)
www.stonecare.com

U.S. Consumer Product Safety Commission
www.cpsc.gov

U.S. Environmental Protection Agency (EPA)
www.epa.gov

U.S. Food and Drug Administration (FDA)
www.fda.gov

Picture credits

1 The home of the artist Lou Kenlock, Oxfordshire Ph: Catherine Gratwicke. 2 A family home in west London by Webb Architects and Cave Interiors Ph: Polly Wreford. 3 Ph: Caroline Arber. 4 Beauty Point & Coast House available as locations from www.beachstudios.co.uk Ph: Polly Wreford. 5 Cathie Curran Architects Ph: Polly Wreford. 6 The home of Charlie and Alex Willcock and family in West Sussex Ph: Polly Wreford. 7a Ph: Claire Richardson. 7c Ph: Debi Treloar. 7b Ph: Winfried Heinze. 8 The home of Anne Bjelke hapelbloggen.blogspot.no Ph: Catherine Gratwicke. 9a Ph: Debi Treloar. 9b Ph: Winfried Heinze. 10 Pauline's apartment in Paris, designed by Marianne Evennou www.marianne-evennou.com Ph: Rachel Whiting. 11l Ph: Debi Treloar. 11c An apartment in New York designed by Belmont Freeman Architects Ph: Polly Wreford. 11r Designed by Stéphane Garotin and Pierre Emmanuel Martin of Maison Hand in Lyon Ph: Rachel Whiting. 12l The family home of Louise Kamman Riising, co-owner of hey-home.dk Ph: Rachel Whiting. 12r Foster Cabin designed by Dave Coote www.beachstudios.co.uk Ph: Polly Wreford. 13 The home of the stylist and writer Sara Emslie in London Ph: Rachel Whiting. 14 Home of Rose Hammick and Andrew Treverton, www.marmoraroad.co.uk Ph: Polly Wreford. 15a Ph: Mark Scott. 15c The cabin of Hanne Borge and her family in Norway Ph: Catherine Gratwicke. 15b The home of Anna Parker Ph: Polly Wreford. 16 Ph: Sandra Lane. 17 Ph: Andrew Wood. 18l Ph: Lucinda Symons. 18r Baileys baileyshome.com Tel: 01989 561931 Ph: Debi Treloar. 19a Stenhuset Antikhandel shop, café and B&B in Stockamollan, Sweden Ph: Polly Wreford. 19b Ph: Lucinda Symons. 20al Ph: Polly Wreford. 20l and c and br Ph: Simon Brown. 21 Ph: Caroline Arber. 22 Bruno et Michèle Viard: location-en-luberon.com Ph: Polly Wreford. 23l Sharon & Paul Mrozinski's home in Bonnieux, France, www.marstonhouse.com Ph: Debi Treloar. 23r Ph: Dan Duchars. 26 The home of stylist Emma Persson Lagerberg Ph: Polly Wreford. 27 Ph: Mark Scott. 28 A family home in London designed by Marion Lichtig Ph: Polly Wreford. 29a The Los Angeles home of Adam and Kate Blackman, www.blackmancruz.com Ph: Catherine Gratwicke. 29b Ph: Mark Scott. 30a Beauty Point & Coast House available as locations from www.beachstudios.co.uk Ph: Polly Wreford. 30bl Ph: David Montgomery. 30br Ph: Mark Scott. 31 Designed by Jane Cumberbatch, www.purestyleonline.com Ph: Lisa Cohen. 32 Ph: Mark Lohman. 34a The home of Matt & Jax Fothergill in Shropshire Ph: Jan Baldwin. 34b Ph: Mark Lohman. 35 Sophie Conran's home in London Ph: Catherine Gratwicke. 37 The designers Piet & Karin Boon's home near Amsterdam, www.pietboon.nl Ph: Lisa Cohen. 38 background Ph: Debi Treloar. 38 insert Bryn Eglur is available for holiday rental at www.thewelshhouse.org Ph: Debi Treloar. 40a The home of Erica Farjo & David Slade Ph: Catherine Gratwicke. 40b A house in Stockholm, Sweden Ph: Andrew Wood. 41 Ritva Puotila's summerhome in Finland Ph: Paul Ryan. 42l Ph: Debi Treloar. 42r The London Loft of Andrew Weaving of Century, www.centuryd.com Ph: Andrew Wood. 43a Ph: Catherine Gratwicke. 43b Lykkeoglykkeliten.blogspot.com Ph: Debi Treloar. 44 Home of Rose Hammick and Andrew Treverton, www.marmoraroad.co.uk Ph: Polly Wreford. 46a The home of 'créatrice' and designer Stine Weirsøe Holm in Malmö Ph: Debi Treloar. 46b Family Ponsa-Hemmings home from xo-inmyroom.com Ph: Rachel Whiting. 47 "La villa des Ombelles" the family home of Jean-Marc Dimanche Chairman of V.I.T.R.I.O.L. agency www.vitriol-factory.com Ph: Debi Treloar. 48 A family home in London designed by Marion Lichtig Ph: Polly Wreford. 49 New Cross – location to hire through www.beachstudios.co.uk Ph: Polly Wreford. 50 The home of Anne Bjelke hapelbloggen.blogspot.no Ph: Catherine Gratwicke. 51al Ph: Jan Baldwin. 51bl Upper East Side Townhouse in New York designed by DiDonno Associates Architects, P.C. Ph: Christopher Drake. 51r The South London home of designer Virginia Armstrong of roddy&ginger Ph: Polly Wreford. 52 The home of the artist Lou Kenlock, Oxfordshire Ph: Catherine Gratwicke. 53ar The home of Britt, Jurgen and Mascha Ph: Rachel Whiting. 53cr The London home of designer Kathy Dalwood www.kathydalwood.com and artist Justin Mortimer www.justinmortimer.co.uk Ph: Debi Treloar. 53br Sophie Conran's home in London Ph: Catherine Gratwicke. 54al Ph: Lisa Cohen. 54ac Ph: Mark Scott. 54ar Baileys www.baileyshome.com Tel : 01989 561931 Ph: Debi Treloar. 55 Designed by Jane Cumberbatch, www.purestyleonline.com Ph: Lisa Cohen. 56 The family home of Fiona and Alex Cox of www.coxandcox.co.uk Ph: Polly Wreford. 57 Naja Lauf Ph: Paul Massey. 58 A house in Lincolnshire designed by Lulu Carter Design Ph: Jan Baldwin. 59a Ph: Steve Painter. 59b Ph: Chris Everad. 60al Ph: Polly Wreford. 60bl Ph: Edina van der Wyck. 60r The family home in Norfolk of Laura & Fred Ingrams of Arie & Ingrams Design Ph: Debi Treloar. 61 The family home of Katie & Alex Clarke, the owners of the boutique hotel The George in Rye Ph: Polly Wreford. 62 Alfredo Paredes and Brad Goldfarb's loft in Tribeca, New York designed by Michael Neumann Architecture Ph: Jan Baldwin. 64 Florence & John Pearse's apartment in London Ph: Winfried Heinze. 65 Ph: James Merrell. 67 The home of Jenny Atherton, co-owner of Lavender Room in Brighton Ph: Debi Treloar. 68 The home of the artist Lou Kenlock, Oxfordshire Ph: Catherine Gratwicke. 69 Ph: Mark Scott. 71 House in Vaud, Switzerland Ph: Debi Treloar. 72l Ph: Catherine Gratwicke. 72r Oliver Heath and Katie Weiner – sustainable architecture, interior and jewellery design Ph: Catherine Gratwicke. 73 Ph: Simon Brown. 74 Lykkeoglykkeliten.blogspot.com Ph: Debi Treloar. 75a The home of Susan Callery, owner of Greenlane Gallery, in Dingle www.greenlanegallery.com Ph: James Fennell. 75b Ph: Debi Treloar. 76 Ph: Simon Brown. 77 www.aureliemathigot.com Ph: Debi Treloar. 78 Ph: Martin Brigdale. 79a Ph: Debi Treloar. 79b Ph: Lucinda Symons. 80 The home of James and Maria Backhouse in London Ph: Debi Treloar. 81a The South London home of designer Virginia Armstrong of roddy&ginger Ph: Polly Wreford. 81b The designer Clare Teed's home in Hampton, www.sashawaddell.com Ph: Lisa Cohen. 82 New Cross – location to hire through www.beachstudios.co.uk Ph: Polly Wreford. 83al Foster Cabin designed by Dave Coote www.beachstudios.co.uk Ph: Polly Wreford. 83bl Ph: Debi Treloar. 83r The South London home of designer Virginia Armstrong of roddy&ginger Ph: Polly Wreford. 84 The home of Elina Tripoliti and Mark Rachovides in London Ph: Debi Treloar. 85 Photographer Joanna Vestey and her husband Steve Brooks' home in Cornwall Ph: Jan Baldwin. 86 A family home in London designed by Marion Lichtig. Ph: Polly Wreford 87 The family home of Fiona and Alex Cox of www.coxandcox.co.uk Ph: Polly Wreford. 88 The family home of the interior decorator Mary Jane Russell of 'Town & Country', Cork Ph: James Fennell. 89 Constanze von Unruh's house in London Ph: Jan Baldwin. 90 and 92 Retrouvius owners, Adam Hills and Maria Speake's apartment in London Ph: Debi Treloar. 93 The family home of Sarah and Mark Benton in Rye Ph: Polly Wreford. 94 Signe Bindslev Henriksen of Space Architecture and Design Ph: Winfried Heinze. 95a Ph: Kristin Perers. 95b Ph: Mark Lohman. 96 stylist Rose Hammick and architect Andrew Treverton's home in London Ph: Dan Duchars. 97l Holly Jolliffe 97c Ph: Polly Wreford. 97r Available for location hire at shootspaces.com Ph: Debi Treloar. 98–99 Ph: Andrew Wood. 102a Ph: Mark Scott. 102b The family home of Gina Portman of Folk at Home www.folkathome.com Ph: Catherine Gratwicke. 103 Ph: Polly Wreford. 104 The designer Nina Hartmann's home in Sweden, www.vintagebynina.com Ph: Lisa Cohen. 105a Ph: Claire Richardson. 105b Ph: Winfried Heinze. 106 Ph: Isobel Wield. 107a Ph: Kristin Perers. 107b Ph: Winfried Heinze. 108a Ph: Polly Wreford. 108b Ph: Holly Jolliffe. 109 background Ph: Chris Tubbs. 109 insert Ph: Mark Lohman. 110 Baileys www.baileyshome.com Tel : 01989 561931 Ph: Debi Treloar. 111a Rose Hammick and architect Andrew Treverton's home in London Ph: Dan Duchars. 111b The home of Vidar and Ingrid Aune Westrum Ph: Debi Treloar. 112l Anna Mcdougall's London Home Ph: Lisa Cohen. 112c Ph: Andrew Wood. 112r Ph: Paul Massey. 113 The home of Jeanette Lunde Frydogdesign.blogspot.com Ph: Debi Treloar. 114 Ph: Polly Wreford. 115 Ph: Lucinda Symons. 116 Ph: Mark Scott. 117 Paul & Claire's beach house, East Sussex. Design www.davecoote.com; Location to hire through www.beachstudios.co.uk Ph: Polly Wreford. 118l The home of Jean-Louis Fages and Matthieu Ober in Nimes Ph: Claire Richardson. 118r ph: Paul Ryan. 119 New Cross – location to hire through www.beachstudios.co.uk Ph: Polly Wreford. 120 Ph: William Reavell. 121a Ph: William Reavell. 121b Ph: Steve Painter. 122l Ph: Steve Painter. 122c Ph: Peter Cassidy. 122 r Ph: Peter Cassidy. 123 William Peers & Sophie Poklewski Koziell Ph: Jan Baldwin. 124 Ph: Martin Brigdale. 125 Ph: Steve Painter. 126 Ph: Kate Whitaker. 127 Ph: Winfried Heinze. 128 Ph: Martin Brigdale. 129 Ph: Steve Painter. 131 Ph: Simon Brown. 132 Ph: Andrew Wood. 133 Ph: William Reavell. 134 Ph: Ian Wallace. 135 The home of Yvonne Eijkenduijn of www.yvestown.com in Belgium Ph: Catherine Gratwicke. 144 Ph: Dan Duchars. 145l Ph: Jan Baldwin. 145r Ph: Steve Painter. 146 The home of Kamilla Bryiel and Christian Permin in Copenhagen Ph: Winfried Heinze. 147a and c Ph: Steve Painter. 147b Ph: Kate Whitaker. 148–149 Ph Debi Treloar. 150–151 Ph: David Brittain. 157 Andrew Hoffman & Alex Bates' home on Fire Island Ph: Earl Carter. 160 The family home of Nicky Sanderson, the co-owner of Lavender Room in Brighton, East Sussex Ph: Debi Treloar. **Endpapers** The family home in Denmark of Tine Kjeldsen and Jacob Fossum owners of www.tinekhome.dk Ph: Polly Wreford.

Index

Bibliography

Food storage

Food storage guidelines chart from *The Food Keeper: A Consumer Guide to Food Quality and Safe Handling*, developed by the FMI, Washington, D.C., with Cornell University Institute of Food Science, Cornell University Extension.

United States Department of Agriculture, Food Safety and Inspection Service. Consumer Information on food safety and other topics. www.usda.gov

Stain Removal

Field, Anne, Michigan State University Extension Specialist. 'Carpet Spot Removal Chart' and 'Identifying Mysterious Stains on Textile Furnishings'. Michigan State University Extension Home Maintenance and Repair. Michigan State University Extension Cooperative Extension. www.msue.msu.edu

Guide to repairing scratches and removing stains on wood

National Wood Flooring Association. 'Caring for Wood Floors', 'An Ounce of Prevention', 'Hot tips on Floor Maintenance', 'Repairing Scratches and Removing Stains'. www.woodfloors.org

Guide to removing stains on stone

Marble Institute of America. 'Stain Removal – Tile Guide' Care and Cleaning for Natural Stone Surfaces www.marble-institute.com

Laundry

ASTM Guide for Care Symbols. 'Standard Guide for Care Symbols for Care Instructions on Textile Products'.

American Society for Testing and Materials (ASTM) 1996. 1997 *Annual Book of ASTM Standards*. www.astm.guide

'Stain Removal Guide' by Dr. Everlyn Johnson, Extension apparel and textiles specialist. University of Mississippi Extension Service. www.msucares.com/pubs/publications/p1400.pdf

General

Berthold-Bond, Annie. *Better Basics for the Home* (Three Rivers Press, 1999).

Edited by Linda Hallam. *Making a Home* (Better Homes and Gardens Books, 2001).

Mendelson, Cheryl. *Home Comforts: the Art and Science of Keeping House* (Scribner, 2005). A thoroughly comprehensive and detailed reference book on housework.

Pinkham, Mary Ellen. *Mary Ellen's Guide to Good Enough Housekeeping* (St. Martin's Griffin, 2002).

The author has made every effort to contact copyright holders; in the event of an inadvertent omission or error, please notify the editorial department at Ryland Peters & Small, 20–21 Jockey's Fields, London WC1R 4BW.